Gertrude Stein

A BIOGRAPHY

Gertrude Stein in her sitting room at 27, rue de Fleurus. Above her head is the portrait Picasso painted of her.

Gertrude Stein
A BIOGRAPHY

by Howard Greenfeld

CROWN PUBLISHERS, INC., NEW YORK

ACKNOWLEDGMENTS

It would have been impossible to write this book without the advice and encouragement of my editor, Norma Jean Sawicki. I would also like to thank Tamara Hovey, Alice Cromie, Maria Tommasi, and David Scholder for their help.

Printed in the United States of America
Library of Congress Catalog Card Number: 72-92385
ISBN: 0-517-50260-7
Published simultaneously in Canada by General Publishing Company Limited
First Edition

The text of this book is set in 12 pt. Palatino.
The illustrations are B/W halftones.

To Freda Barry Brown

Gertrude Stein

A BIOGRAPHY

Chapter 1

FOR MANY YEARS, DURING THE FIRST HALF OF THE TWENTIETH century, the small, two-story pavilion at 27, rue de Fleurus was one of the best-known addresses in all of Paris. At one time or another, almost every important writer or artist in the western world passed through its doors. Since the French capital itself was the center of the world's cultural activities, 27, rue de Fleurus assumed international importance.

On Saturday evenings the doors of the four-room pavilion at the back of the courtyard were open to all, and over a period of thirty-five years the distinguished visitors continued to take advantage of the open invitation to meet one another and exchange ideas; to look at a fabulous collection of paintings; or, especially, to meet the fascinating American woman whose magnetic presence gave life to 27, rue de Fleurus.

Her name was Gertrude Stein, and she was one of the most original and compelling figures in the world of art and literature for almost half a century. Though her position in that world was a complex and somewhat mysterious one, she became a reigning empress within it.

The court over which she presided was held in her enormous studio, which dwarfed the rest of her apartment on Paris's Left Bank. It was heated by a huge iron stove and was filled with heavy pieces of Italian Renaissance furniture, including a large table topped with an inkstand and several notebooks, all neatly arranged, their covers illustrated with fanciful scenes of earthquakes and explorations, the kind used by French schoolchildren for their homework. The chairs scattered throughout the studio were also Italian Renaissance, good to look at but uncomfortable to sit in.

Visitors to the studio might have complained of the clutter and the uncomfortable seating, but no one questioned the taste and authority that were evident in the selection of the marvelous paintings that hung two and three deep on the walls of the vast room. It was a collection that could rival that of many museums, with masterpieces by El Greco, Manet, Renoir, Gauguin, and Cézanne hung alongside works by the modern masters Matisse and Picasso.

Matisse and Picasso themselves were among the many painters who often came to the rue de Fleurus. Others were Georges Braque, Georges Rouault, Marie Laurencin, and Juan Gris. Among the many writers who frequented Miss Stein's salon were Guillaume Apollinaire, Ernest Hemingway, Sherwood Anderson, and F. Scott Fitzgerald. But there is no end to the list of the interested or the merely curious who came to visit Gertrude Stein. "By nine o'clock there were so many people that the party had to overflow into the apartment from the studio, which had become too cramped," wrote Fernande Olivier, Picasso's mistress for many years. "There was always a mixture of artists, bohemians and professional people, and, of course, foreigners. It was an odd spectacle—this assortment of people from quite different worlds, all talking about art and literature. . . . The evenings we spent there were sometimes gay, sometimes not, but they were always stimulating."

For most of those Saturday evenings, Gertrude Stein

would sit straight in a magnificent high-backed Renaissance chair, attentively observing everything and everyone around her. More often than not, during her first years at the rue de Fleurus, she was silent, speaking only formal phrases to those who approached her. Every once in a while, and seemingly without reason, she would burst into laughter, a hearty, infectious, engaging laugh.

As the years went by and her self-confidence grew, she spoke more, strongly dominating the salon. People came not out of curiosity, but to pay homage to this woman with the squat figure—shaped as if she were wearing a hoopskirt from neck to knees. Her chair came to resemble a throne. Gertrude Stein had become world famous, but, ironically, many people did not know why.

Today, many years after her death, her name remains a familiar one, and with the passage of time it has become easier to assess the reasons for her influence and power in the world of art and literature. They may be found in the life and work of this unique woman who helped shape the intellectual life of the twentieth century.

Chapter 2

WHEN DANIEL AND AMELIA STEIN MARRIED IN 1864, THEY decided that they would have five children. By 1871, they had reached their goal, but tragedy struck, and two of the children died. Keeping to their original plan, they then had two more children: Leo, who was born in 1872, and Gertrude, born in 1874.

Gertrude later admitted that though she and Leo never discussed the matter very much, it did make them feel odd. What would have happened to them if the other children hadn't died? But the question was too puzzling and confusing to answer: it was best forgotten.

At the time of Gertrude's birth, Daniel was in the wholesale wool business with his brother Solomon in Allegheny, Pennsylvania, near Pittsburgh. However, just one year after the baby's birth, the brothers argued and gave up the business. Solomon moved to New York, while Daniel decided to take his family to Vienna, where he had good business contacts. So it was that Gertrude took her first trip to Europe, where she was to spend the best part of her life.

But Daniel Stein was a restless man, and shortly after settling his wife and five children in Vienna, he returned to the United States. Amelia, a simple, gentle woman, felt lonely in the Austrian capital, however, without her husband, and in 1878 she took the children to live in Passy, on the outskirts of Paris. It was at that time that Gertrude had her first taste of French life, which she always remembered fondly. She went to kindergarten there, she spoke French, she learned to eat soup for breakfast and mutton and spinach for lunch. She loved to watch the

Unidentified woman, Bertha, Simon, tutor, Michael, Gertrude, and Leo.

free-spirited French cats, and she ate the best potatoes of her life. As the baby of the family—her brother Michael was thirteen, Simon was ten, Leo was six, and her sister Bertha was eight—she was pampered and spoiled.

In 1879, Daniel decided to bring his family back to the

United States, and Gertrude spent a year with her mother's parents in Baltimore. Her routine there was a bit more rigid since her grandparents were strict Orthodox Jews, but she fit into it beautifully. She enjoyed being fussed over, this time by adoring aunts and uncles.

But the following year when Gertrude was six her life began to change. Daniel's dream had always been to live in California and, having found a good position there with a cable car company, he moved the family to Oakland, near San Francisco. There they lived in comfort, in a large house in the country. There were governesses and music lessons and the children had their clothes made to order. Nonetheless, the home was often a tense one. Daniel was a nervous, domineering man, and he ruled his children with an iron hand. Discipline was severely imposed, tempered only by Amelia's kindness and love.

In Oakland, Gertrude entered the first grade where she was an average student. Her real pleasures came from exploring the joys and surprises of nature, and from reading, which she began to do with great enthusiasm. In spite of the somewhat tense atmosphere in the home, life during those first years in California seemed simple and beautiful.

All this came to an end when, in 1885, Amelia Stein was afflicted with cancer. Soon she was bedridden, and her influence in the family quickly diminished. Daniel reluctantly became a part-time nurse to his wife. He was restless and explosive, unable to unify the family, so the children had to band together. Michael was shy and gentle and intelligent, but, being almost ten years older than

Gertrude, the two had little in common at that point. Simon, according to his younger sister, was fat and stupid, and Bertha was dull, so Gertrude and Leo were inevitably drawn together. Finding little happiness in their home, they found consolation outside of it. They both loved to walk and to talk and to take long bicycle trips. And, above all, they shared a passion for reading.

Their real home became the library—there was an excellent free library in Oakland and several very good ones in San Francisco. Gertrude read everything in sight: her favorites were the British writers—Swift, Burke, Defoe, Scott, Burns, Bunyan, Wordsworth, Fielding, and Smollett. Her favorite novel was Richardson's *Clarissa*, and for her the greatest of all writers was Shakespeare. In fact, at the age of eight, she attempted to write a play in imitation of his tragedies. Her reading was varied—evolution was a subject of passionate interest to her, and she devoured any available works by Darwin or Huxley. Even the *Congressional Record* stimulated her, and she read it avidly. She was learning to love her language and, as she later wrote, she "lived continually with the rhythms of the English language." French, too, was not forgotten. In San Francisco there was a lively interest in France, and Gertrude admired the French fashions shown there, enjoyed the visiting French theatre—she even saw the great actress Sarah Bernhardt perform—and she came to know many French residents of San Francisco. Her adolescence, shared closely with Leo, was as rich outside the home as it was unsettled within it.

When Gertrude was fourteen years old, her mother

died. The young girl had already become reconciled to the idea of a girlhood without a mother, but with Amelia's death any semblance of order disappeared from the home. Daniel was seldom home and when he was he became increasingly tyrannical. The children were given orders without understanding, material comforts without affection. Total chaos reigned in the household: there were no regular hours and no family meals. To Gertrude and Leo, Daniel Stein represented power without reason, and they increasingly rebelled, openly fighting their father while leading their real lives outside the home. They were sure that the true meaning of life was to be found in the books they so avidly read. As she passionately read every volume she could find, Gertrude began to worry that in time she would have read everything there was to read. This thought threw her into panic: a world without more books to read would be unlivable.

She knew, however, that life without a father would not be unlivable, so Daniel's death in 1891 caused her little pain. It happened suddenly and unexpectedly: one morning he didn't come down from his room for breakfast. The children called to him, but there was no answer; they tried to open his door, but it was locked. Finally, Leo went out of the house and climbed up to the window. When he entered the room, he found his father had died in his sleep of a heart attack.

To Gertrude this was no great loss; as she herself said, she had always found her father "depressing." Indeed, his death gave her a sense of freedom she had never before known. Michael, now twenty-six years old, assumed full responsibility. He had studied at Johns Hopkins University in Baltimore and had returned to San Francisco to work at the cable car company with his father. At Daniel's death there was a little money left, but Michael was earning well at his job. More important, he supplied to his younger sister a tenderness and understanding her mother had been too ill and her father too selfish to give her. She enjoyed his company, and Michael encouraged her in her love of books and theatre, providing her also with the economic stability to pursue whatever goals she chose.

However, Gertrude was still uncertain as to what these goals were. In 1892, Leo, always her closest friend, had gone off to study at Harvard; he had been her guide and mentor through the world of literature and art and music. Thus, it seemed only natural that she should follow him a year later and enter the women's branch of Harvard, then known as Harvard Annex, today known as Radcliffe. She had not enjoyed school in Oakland—the only thing that interested her was diagramming sentences. Yet in ways she was far better equipped than most students entering the university at the time. She spoke and read some French and German, which she had learned during her years abroad, in addition to which her many hours at the library had given her ample background to continue her studies.

Harvard was alive with activity in 1893 when Gertrude Stein began her studies there. She was a short, dumpy girl, yet her face was warm and soft, and her overall appearance—perhaps because of her open personality and

Gertrude (*upper left*) at Radcliffe with friends.

obvious intelligence—was attractive. She described her
face as "singularly attractive, largely because puzzling."
Upon arrival, she lined the walls of her room with books;
they reached to the ceiling. Her wardrobe was another
matter—it consisted of drab clothing, and its most out-

standing item was a straw sailor's hat with faded ribbons hanging from it.

She entered into the bustling intellectual life with vigor. The Harvard–Radcliffe faculty at the time included some of the most brilliant teachers and thinkers in the world, and Gertrude took full advantage of them.

Most important to her were the courses in philosophy. She was able to study with the outstanding Spanish-born George Santayana, a philosopher of materialism who taught that reality consists only of matter. In contrast there was a stimulating course in metaphysics, given by the California-born, German-educated Josiah Royce, a leading idealist who believed that it was possible to prove ultimate truths. Another fascinating mind available to the young girl was that of George Herbert Palmer, with whom she studied logic.

But there were two men who were of even greater importance to the maturing Gertrude Stein. One was Hugo Münsterberg, a German professor who had come to Harvard to direct a new psychological laboratory, one especially equipped for experimental psychology. Psychology fascinated her. In her very early days at college, she had been most interested in learning about herself, but soon her interest expanded to the understanding of others, for which the study of psychology was essential. Her enthusiasm led her to become an outstanding student. By the end of her second year at college, the great Münsterberg wrote to her: "I thank you above all for the model-work you have done in my laboratory . . . you were to me the ideal student!" Later, when the German psychologist wrote an article describing his teaching years in America, he used Gertrude as his example of the perfect student.

At Münsterberg's suggestion, she conducted an interesting series of experiments to show that a "normal" person could perform certain acts completely foreign to him under special circumstances. Her partner in these experiments was Leon Solomons, a brilliant young graduate student, also from northern California. The intensely serious and intellectual Solomons was Gertrude's closest friend throughout her stay at Harvard. His tragic, premature death in 1900 upset her greatly, and she later wrote that the young man had "left a definite mark" on her life.

The two students themselves were the subjects for their experiments: one would hold a pencil and write down a series of words while the other read a story aloud. The results of this writing while distracted were of such interest that they were published in the important *Psychological Review* under the title "Normal Motor Automatism." Later on, while still at Radcliffe, Gertrude conducted further experiments in this area, without the help of Leon Solomons. Instead of limiting herself to the reactions of two people, she used a sampling of almost one hundred men and women, whose "automatic writing" consisted not of words but of rhythmic movements such as circles, figure eights, and curves. Instead of having stories read to them as a distraction, they were encouraged to converse or give in to daydreams while writing. The results of this work were also published in *Psychological*

Review, under the title "Cultivated Motor Automatism."

Thus, it was through Hugo Münsterberg that her work was first publicly recognized. Yet the major influence on her future was to be another man, perhaps the most distinguished professor at Harvard, William James. This great psychologist-philosopher's brother was Henry James, a novelist whom Gertrude deeply respected. William James himself was to become the founder of the pragmatic school of philosophy. More important for Gertrude, James too was concerned with the use of language under unusual circumstances. While under the influence of nitrous oxide, this usually rational philosopher wrote such phrases as "There are no differences but differences of degree between different degrees of difference and no difference," a kind of writing that would find echoes in Gertrude's later work.

William James was everything that a professor should be: he had a brilliant mind and a dynamic, forceful personality—impulsive, imaginative, and colorful. He demanded that his students keep their minds open to every idea and current of thought. For him, Gertrude Stein, always alert and interested, was the ideal student as she had been for Münsterberg. At all times she was ready to explore every possibility and to argue every point, though sometimes not by logic, but—in her own words—"by loudness of voice, number of words and violence of manner." Her fairly frequent emotional outbursts never bothered James, however, and he admired both her intelligence and her passion in expressing it. Gertrude's feeling for her professor approached adoration. For one college theme

Professor William James.

she wrote: "Is life worth living? Yes, a thousand times yes when the world still holds such spirits as Prof. James. . . . His is a strong sane noble personality reacting truly on all experience that life has given him. He is a man take him for all in all."

No experience at college could match the stimulation of studying with William James, yet when it came time for the final examination in his course, Gertrude was at a loss. For reasons she could not explain, she was unable to write the answers to his questions. Instead, she penned a note to her professor:

Dear Professor James. I am so sorry but really I do not feel a bit like an examination paper in philosophy today.

And she walked out of the classroom.

William James was known for his informality, his sense of individual freedom, so it was not truly surprising that the next day Gertrude received the following note from him:

Dear Miss Stein. I understand perfectly how you feel. I often feel like that myself.

At the bottom of the note was her grade, the highest given to any student.

During her years at college, Gertrude's primary interests were psychology and philosophy. She did well in her one history course, but poorly in French 2 which consisted of elementary French reading from La Fontaine to Balzac. Most surprising, she received a C for the only English class she took, a sophomore course in composition. Her professor, a noted teacher, poet, and playwright named William Vaughn Moody, did find that some of her writing was "interesting," showed some humor and "considerable emotional intensity." However, he was alarmed by her frequent misuses of grammar and her poor sentence structure. He was not the only one to be disturbed by her seemingly sloppy writing. Leon Solomons had written about one of her reports: "You ought to be ashamed of yourself for the careless manner in which you have written it up." There is evidence of this carelessness in most of her college themes, and it can probably be explained by the same "emotional intensity" for which Moody had commended her. Gertrude was intense and little concerned with the form in which she expressed her feelings at the time. Whatever the reasons for her sloppy writing, it did not seem likely that her talents would be directed toward the field of literature. It was in no way a promising beginning for a writer, but then, while at college, Gertrude never showed any interest in becoming one.

The years at Radcliffe were generally happy ones. At times, thinking of herself as a Westerner, she felt foreign in the midst of the cold New England temperament at Cambridge, but she had a lively extracurricular life and seemed to have no difficulty in making friends, even though she often thought of herself as a somewhat dreary bookworm. Leo was there, of course, and they continued to be very close, but she also made a life of her own. Her informality fit perfectly into the informality of student life. She went to art galleries and to operas and to the theatre, sometimes as often as twice a day. She became secretary of the Philosophy Club and was active in the Idlers Club, which produced playlets. Her energy and enthusiasm for debate knew no bounds, and her interest in outdoor life was satisfied by long bicycle rides, boat rides, and picnics with friends. During the summers, she either visited Michael in San Francisco or traveled through Europe with Leo.

She was a passionate and gifted young woman, but by the time her Radcliffe years were coming to an end, she was still in search of a direction, an outlet for her talents. She felt inside her that she had something special to offer, that she was in some way destined to become immortal. "I want to be historical," she wrote, but she had yet to find a means toward achieving her ambitious goal.

As she was about to leave college, she discussed the problem of her future with William James, who advised her to continue her studies in either philosophy or psychology. For the former, she would need to study higher mathematics, which had never interested her; but for psychology she would need a medical education, for which, through her studies in biology and chemistry, she had shown a far greater aptitude.

Once again, then, she followed Leo who was already studying biology at Johns Hopkins in Baltimore. Many members of her mother's family also lived there, so she applied for admission to the newly opened School of Medicine at Hopkins. The opening of the school had been delayed for lack of funds, funds which were eventually raised by daughters of four of the trustees. At the end of the nineteenth century, it was most unusual for a woman to want to become a doctor, so it was fitting that one of the women who had raised the money for the school made her contribution with the condition that women receive unprejudiced instruction in the study of medicine. Gertrude took advantage of this early example of women's asserting their rights, as did many other bright young American women at the time: the way to study at an outstanding medical school would no longer be barred to them because of their sex. And Johns Hopkins was one of the finest schools in the country, its faculty headed by Sir William Osler, a leading Canadian physician and teacher, who attracted to the college an unusually brilliant faculty. The opportunities for learning medicine there were as great as those for learning philosophy and psychology had been at Harvard.

Gertrude was happy to be back in Baltimore—she liked the city and its people. She enjoyed her first two years in medical school; they were a challenge, and laboratory work which took up most of her time had always fascinated her. She also enjoyed her role as a woman pioneer in the field of medicine, and in her second year at medical school she addressed a group of Baltimore women on the necessity of a college education for women as a means toward their eventual independence. A woman, she felt, should not be treated as a commodity, groomed for nothing but marriage. Through higher education, women could learn to exist independent of men. In the process, she went on, education "does not tend to unsex but to rightly sex women."

Nonetheless, Gertrude herself was not willing to carry on the battle through her own medical school education. During her last two years at Hopkins, she lost all interest in and enthusiasm for her work. She felt restricted by the special discipline involved, felt there was too little room for her imagination. She was bored as she had never

Gertrude at Johns Hopkins.

been before, and she hated much of what she was forced to do—including delivering nine babies, which was one part of her studies. Her professors were horrified as her lack of interest manifested itself in increasingly poor grades. How could such an obviously brilliant young woman do so badly? She plodded on, but only for lack of anything else to do, until her last year, which was a total disaster. She failed four subjects: ophthalmology and otology; dermatology; laryngology and rhinology; and obstetrics.

The faculty had no choice but to recommend that she not be given a degree, but they granted her one more chance if she agreed to take a summer course to make up for the subjects she had failed. After giving the matter a minimum of thought, she made up her mind. Under no condition would she continue medical school; a degree didn't interest her, nor did the practice of medicine. Indeed, she even thanked one professor for having failed her, for stopping her from going ahead in what she felt would have been a dull and useless profession.

One of the women who had donated so much money to the school was furious when Gertrude dropped out; she thought she had shamed her sex. And Marion Walker, a very close friend of Gertrude's from Radcliffe, pleaded with her: "Gertrude, Gertrude, remember the cause of women." Gertrude, exasperated, replied: "But you don't know what it is to be bored."

Gertrude was determined that boredom would not be permitted in her life. Though she had still not made any concrete plans for the future after the bad experience at Hopkins, she decided to spend the summer in Europe with Leo. He, too, had failed to complete his courses at Johns Hopkins and, at the end of his third year there, had precipitously left for Italy: he wanted to write a book on the Italian painter Mantegna and would write it in Florence. However, his interest in the subject dwindled; in fact, he had too many interests and was unable to concentrate on one. He drew and played the violin and was a passionate visitor to art museums throughout Europe. His tastes were varied and extended from Rembrandt, Rubens, Leonardo, Giotto, and Goya on the one hand, to Dutch tiles, Japanese prints and Renaissance furniture on the other. Though personally confused and indecisive, he remained a perfect traveling companion for Gertrude. He knew where to take his sister and how to guide and direct her tastes. She looked up to him with respect and admiration and followed him unquestioningly.

So it was a good trip, as enjoyable as the one they had taken in 1901 to Tangiers and Spain and Paris, but when fall came she had still not made up her mind as to what to do with her future, which path to take which would lead her to becoming "historical." She was tempted to stay in Europe with Leo, but there was a possibility of doing extensive brain research in Baltimore, work that was in ways related to the studies in psychology she had pursued at Radcliffe, and she decided to see if such a specialization was suited to her.

At first, her studies interested her, but once again her enthusiasm died out in a short time and by spring she had decided to abandon science once and for all. Against the advice of friends and relatives, she sold her medical books and sailed for Italy.

There she traveled through the enchanting hill towns of Umbria and Tuscany, always guided by Leo, after which she went with her brother to his home near Florence. Together they spent long hours at *I Tatti*, the magnificent villa of Bernard Berenson, the noted art historian and collector. Gertrude, as always, enjoyed life in and

21

around Florence, but Leo was beginning to feel restless, closed in by the smallness of the city. He wanted to move on, and his choice of a place to stay was London.

In September of 1902, he rented an apartment on London's Bloomsbury Square where Gertrude joined him; they planned to stay there through the spring. Bernard Berenson came to England, too, and largely through him Gertrude had a chance to meet some of the most important figures in the world of British literature, among them the novelist Israel Zangwill and the then-young mathematician and philosopher Bertrand Russell. She spoke to them of her problems, of her doubts concerning what to do with the rest of her life, and where to do it. Russell was shocked that Gertrude and Leo would even consider the possibility of returning to America; for him Americans had "closed minds," and the climate there was hardly one in which serious thought could flourish. But Gertrude defended her country and maintained that wherever she chose to live, she would remain an American. She had been formed by America, her language was American, and it would always be impossible for her to reject so much of herself, which would necessarily be the case if she rejected America. As for Leo, he even wrote to a friend that eventually "Gertrude and I will retire to Connecticut or Duxbury or somewhere and live happily ever after."

Wherever she decided to live, Gertrude was certain it would not be London. She found the city cold and gloomy. The only pleasures there were in the reading room of the British Museum, near their apartment, where she spent hours on end, reading everything in sight. Her special interests again were Shakespeare and the Elizabethans, and she discovered and enthusiastically read the works of the sixteenth century writer Robert Greene, as well as the novels of Anthony Trollope. As she read, she took notes, reminders of those works that had given her the greatest satisfaction. Happily, she realized too that her fears in Oakland had been unfounded: looking at the gigantic shelves of the library of the British Museum, she knew there would always be more books for her to read.

Yet London was not the city for her. As she wandered around the streets, she found them "infinitely depressing and dismal." Everything reminded her of Dickens, and Dickens frightened her. She felt melancholy and lonesome, and on February 3, 1903, she sailed for New York.

Once she reached there, she made arrangements to take an apartment with friends near Columbia University. There she gave further thought to her future plans. Medicine was out, as were all purely scientific pursuits; they were too limiting and didn't allow her to inject her own personality into her work. Yet psychology, the study of the human behavior, continued to fascinate her, so she decided to try writing books, through which she might understand and explain the motives and behavior of human beings. Books, utilizing both her interest in people and her desire to explore the uses of her language, seemed to her a likely answer to her search for a road to immortality. Her first project was to write about the Stein family in New York; the theme of a traditional German-Jewish family transplanted to the United States seemed

Claribel Cone, Gertrude Stein, and Etta Cone, Florence, 1903.

to her a rich one. In addition, she wanted to begin work on a short novel, one more directly related to her own experience.

She worked hard throughout the winter and spring, and, when summer came, there came with it another chance to join Leo in Europe. He too had left London and had decided to return to America, but before doing so, while dining with the cellist Pablo Casals, he had a vision of himself as a painter. To become a painter a man had to live in Paris, so he no longer had a choice: he had to settle in the French capital. Through a cousin, a sculptor, he found an apartment. It was at 27, rue de Fleurus, on the edge of Paris's Montparnasse, a quarterly largely inhabited by artists, sculptors, and writers.

Gertrude met him in the summer of 1903, and the two traveled to North Africa, Spain, and Italy, Leo ever the authoritative guide, Gertrude ever the attentive and energetic pupil. At the end of the summer, faced once again with the decision of where to settle, Gertrude made up her mind to stay in Paris. She had always felt happy and free there, and she liked the idea of sharing an apartment with Leo. In addition, Michael and his wife Sarah were living nearby on the rue Madame, in what was once a Protestant church. Michael, having found himself more and more on the side of the growing trade unions—a role hardly befitting an employer—had retired from his San Francisco business in 1902, and moved to Paris shortly thereafter.

As she moved into the apartment at 27, rue de Fleurus, Gertrude felt secure and confident. She was in the city of her choice with the benefits of Leo's intellectual guidance and Michael's financial protection. Under such ideal conditions, she would grow to be "historical."

Chapter 3

HER MIND WAS MADE UP; SHE WOULD BECOME A WRITER, AND Paris seemed the city in which she could best achieve her goals. The temperament of the French people attracted her; they were cordial but distant. France was moving swiftly into the modern age of technology, but there was a deep awareness that technology was not all. In Paris, perhaps more than in any other city of the world, there was a respect for the artist and the writer. The city, too, was drawing to it the most inventive, creative artists of the age—and from all over the world. Most of them were still poor and struggling, but they felt they could best develop their art in the stimulating atmosphere of the French capital.

There was certainly no thought in Gertrude's mind of abandoning America; in fact, one proviso of her move to France was that she return to the United States once a year.

"Everyone who writes is interested in living inside themselves in order to tell what is inside themselves," she believed. "That is why writers have to have two countries, the one where they belong and the one in which they live really. The second one is romantic, it is separate from themselves, it is not real but it is really there."

France, then, became that second country for Gertrude Stein when she moved into the small house on the rue de Fleurus. And, as she later wrote, though America was to remain her country, Paris was to become her hometown.

As soon as she settled down, she began to work again on the novel she had started in New York. It was finished in October 1903, and she gave it the title *Q.E.D.*, the Latin signature for a geometric proof—*Quod Erat Demonstrandum*, meaning "which was to be demonstrated." It seems at the time that only Leo read the book, and Gertrude showed it to no one else for thirty years. Then she retitled it *Things As They Are,* but she still did not want it published; actually the book was printed in a limited edition only after her death and is still known to but a few readers. Her reluctance to expose the book to a large public is difficult to explain. There is the possibility that she felt that it was inferior to and not typical of her later work; there is also the chance that she was embarrassed by its theme, that of three women in the midst of a complicated triangle of love. Whatever the case, it is an interesting psychological study in which the author constantly questions and analyzes the motives and actions of her protagonists. What was demonstrated above all was that Gertrude Stein could indeed write a novel. She not only had the enormous discipline necessary to complete it; she had the talent as well.

These first months in Paris, too, were spent in furnishing Gertrude and Leo's home, the first they had had for many years. Leo had already picked up furniture during his trips to Italy, but more was needed and, with Leo as guide and arbiter of taste, they combed the shops of Paris for interesting pieces.

Most important of all, though, were the walls and the selection of paintings that would hang from them. Here Leo, as elsewhere, was to be the unquestioned judge of what to select. He had studied art, he was well acquainted with the growing museum in San Francisco, and he was himself a painter. In addition, he had become a close friend of the famous connoisseur Bernard Berenson.

The year before the Steins settled in Paris, Berenson had advised Leo to buy a landscape by Paul Cézanne. Leo had gone to Cézanne's dealer, a perceptive and daring but rather short-tempered man named Ambroise Vollard, and purchased not only the recommended landscape, but also paintings by Manet, Daumier, Renoir, and Gauguin. The walls were getting crowded, but there was always room for another painting.

In the winter of 1903–1904, Gertrude fulfilled her pledge; she went back to the United States, remaining there until late spring when she returned to Europe to meet Leo in Florence. In the home of Charles Loeser, the heir to a Brooklyn department store, the Steins were dazzled by an enormous collection of Cézanne. In fact, that summer they spent more time looking at the French painter's works than they did at those masterpieces of Italian painting that hung in Florence's Ufizzi Gallery. By the time they returned to their home in Paris, they were convinced of Cézanne's greatness and proceeded to buy several more of his works. If the money was lacking, they turned to Michael, now their neighbor, upon whom they could always depend for financial help.

Cézanne was not really a discovery, but few collectors were as perceptive as were the Steins at that time in recognizing his true value. The Salon d'Automne of 1904, an annual show of independent painters, was held in the gigantic Grand Palais; as a part of it, there was a one-man exhibition of forty-two of Cézanne's works. Only the young were impressed; the traditional, academic painters and critics were still scornful of the paintings of the man who would one day be recognized as one of the great, innovative masters of all time. One newspaper called his colors "heavy"; another said he merely threw paint on a canvas and then spread it with a comb or toothbrush. Others spoke of his total ignorance of the work of a painter.

But the Steins reacted differently. One painting, a portrait of Cézanne's wife, dressed in gray, seated in a red armchair, particularly fascinated them. It had been lent to the exhibition by Vollard. Day after day, they returned to look at it, in silence. When the Salon closed, Gertrude and Leo went to the dealer, the asked-for amount in hand. Now, Gertrude said, the painting is ours.

In their support of the paintings of Cézanne, these Americans had shown particularly discriminating taste. But they didn't stop with Cézanne.

The next year's Salon d'Automne exhibited the paintings of a new group of painters, whose main concern was not form or content, but the uninhibited use of color. The colors were wild and free—splashes of red and yellow and green and blue, all of them used in a way they had never been used before. There was a Manet exhibition, a showing of the work of Toulouse-Lautrec, both of whom had previously been scorned by critics and public, but the anger once directed at them was no greater than that which greeted the paintings of these color-mad men: Georges Rouault, Georges Braque, André Derain, and

Henri Matisse.

Maurice Vlaminck. Critics called them Les Fauves—the Wild Beasts. And their "leader," wilder than any of them, was Henri Matisse.

Henri Matisse was thirty-six years old; he had painted diligently but had failed to sell a painting in three years. If the critics and public hated the work of the "Wild Beasts," they reserved their greatest hostility for one of Matisse's paintings, *La Femme au Chapeau (The Woman with the Hat)*. So violent were the crowds in their reaction to the Matisse painting that they actually tried to deface it, by scratching off the paint.

As she walked through the Salon, Gertrude was puzzled. The distorted face of the woman, the vermilion eyebrows and green nose shadow seemed natural, normal. She was excited and stimulated by the painting, and Leo agreed that it should become part of their growing collection. But to Leo the price, five hundred francs—then one hundred dollars—seemed high. He made a counteroffer of three hundred francs to the directors of the exhibition. Gertrude warned him that the courageous man who had painted that extraordinary portrait would never agree to reduce the price.

She was right. Matisse, struggling, almost penniless, held out for what he thought his painting was worth.

The Steins, as Gertrude knew they would have to, gave in. They bought their first Matisse for five hundred francs, after which they wanted to meet the painter. Matisse, articulate and friendly, greeted this strange American couple in his studio. There they saw, and bought, other works. Among them was what is possibly the masterpiece of Fauve paintings. It is called *Le Bonheur de Vivre (The Joy of Life)*, an enormous canvas almost six by eight feet, with a series of rose-pink lovers, naked,

Leo, Gertrude, unidentified woman, Sarah, Michael, Allan (*foreground*) in the courtyard at 27, rue de Fleurus, about 1905.

against blue-gray and purple grass, flat, two-dimensional figures forming rhythmic arabesques. At the time, the use of color to express space and movement was revolutionary; to the Steins it was clearly great art. Matisse, for several years, became their close friend. And through them he met Michael and Sarah; the latter became not only his student and disciple but his most important champion in the world of art.

Chapter 4

In 1905, Gertrude met Pablo Picasso; theirs was to be a rich and enduring friendship.

It was Leo, who, in his search for new art, had been told of the work of the then-young Spanish painter. Leo had bought a small Picasso canvas and was anxious to show his sister more of the young man's work. The only place it could be seen was in the "gallery" that Clovis Sagot, a former circus clown, had set up in what used to be a pharmacy. The Steins went there, and Leo was immediately attracted to a large painting showing an adolescent girl holding a basket of bright red flowers, against a smoky blue background. It was called *Girl with a Basket of Flowers*. Leo wanted to buy it at once, but Gertrude didn't. She found the girl too graceless, her legs too ugly, her feet too big. Sagot, anxious to make a sale, suggested a compromise: buy the painting and then cut off the lower part that offended Gertrude. Fortunately, this compromise was not accepted, and Leo's will prevailed. They bought and kept the whole painting for 150 francs, a very small sum at the time.

While Gertrude and Leo were discussing the transaction with Sagot, Picasso himself chanced to come into the shop. The short, strongly built twenty-four-year-old Spaniard closely observed the strange couple—Leo, tall and erect, with his bushy beard and his gold-rimmed eyeglasses, and Gertrude, with her massive body and sculpted head. Both were dressed in corduroy and wore sandals. Gertrude's rich, deep laugh, her forceful personality, and her obviously keen intelligence appealed to the dynamic young man with the black, piercing eyes. He wanted to

Pablo Picasso in St. Raphael, August 1919.

meet the Steins, especially Gertrude, and when they left
the shop, the painter asked Sagot to arrange to have them
come to his studio.

At their first visit to Picasso's, the Steins bought several paintings, but even more important Gertrude and Picasso established a rapport that was to exert a considerable influence on the work of both of them. Theirs was a mutually stimulating friendship. In spite of her initial reservations about Picasso's painting of the adolescent girl, Gertrude soon came to recognize the seeds of genius in the Spaniard's art. There was a tenderness and compassion in his earlier "blue" period and a newly discovered lightness and joy in his "rose" period. More than that, however, at the time she met him Gertrude realized that Picasso was trying to strike out in new directions in his art, as she herself was trying to do in literature. As she observed him progressing toward what would finally develop into an artistic revolution known as Cubism, she —and Leo, too—championed his cause. She introduced the struggling painter to her friends, she spoke of his flowering genius to all who would listen. Intuitively, Gertrude and Leo Stein seemed to recognize that Picasso was to become the greatest painter of the twentieth century.

Shortly after they met, Picasso surprised Gertrude by asking her to pose for him; this was unusual since the artist had not used posed models for many years. However, he saw something special in Gertrude that he wanted to capture on canvas, and she agreed to sit for her portrait.

Over a period of almost three months, there were between eighty and ninety sittings. Gertrude spent nearly every afternoon patiently posing for Picasso. Leaving her home in Montparnasse, she would ride through Paris's winding streets on the top of a horse-drawn bus, which led her to Montmartre, a colorful artists' quarter perched on the top of a hill overlooking the city. She got off at Place Blanche, continuing by foot up the steep rue Lepic, which was lined with food shops, and then continued higher to the rue Ravignan. There, by a flat square covered with chestnut trees, wooden benches, and a fountain, stood the Bateau-Lavoir (the Wash Boat). It was in that lopsided, decrepit wooden building that Cubism was to be born, and it was there that Picasso had his crowded studio.

Each day, in the studio, the scene was the same. Gertrude would sit in a broken-down creaking armchair, and Picasso would take his place on a wobbly kitchen chair, next to the large easel which held the canvas. His palette was a very small one on which there were primarily browns and brownish grays, the colors he felt were suited to his subject. To relieve the inevitable boredom of the long sessions, Picasso would often speak of his life and art; Gertrude was, as always, a receptive, sensitive listener. At other times, Picasso's mistress Fernande Olivier would read aloud the classic *Fables* of La Fontaine to entertain Gertrude. At the end of each day, Gertrude would walk across Paris to her home, accompanied each Saturday by Picasso and Fernande who would stay for dinner and join the increasing number of people who would spend Saturday evenings at the Steins'.

The sittings continued until one day in early summer when Picasso turned to Gertrude and abruptly told her he could no longer see her—and proceeded to paint out the head on which he had worked so long. Something was

Fernande Olivier with unidentified children.

missing, something had gone wrong with his work, and he was dissatisfied with what he had done. It was time for a break, and the two parted for the holidays. Picasso went off to Spain, and Gertrude spent her summer in Italy. When the artist returned, and before seeing his model again, he painted in the head and thereby completed the portrait.

When the young Spaniard presented the finished work to Gertrude, she was delighted, but her friends were dismayed by the masklike severity of the head and complained that it didn't look like her. "Everyone thinks she is not at all like her portrait," Gertrude quotes the artist as saying, "but never mind, in the end she will manage to look just like it." Gertrude understood and knew that Picasso had seen her as she really was, and she treasured the gift for the rest of her life. "He gave me the picture and I was and I still am satisfied with my portrait, for me, it is I, and it is the only reproduction of me which is always I, for me," she later wrote.

The more they saw each other, the more Picasso and Gertrude Stein found they had in common. Seated close together, they would spend hours in conversation, on every possible subject. Gertrude brought the artist the American comic strip *The Katzenjammer Kids*, and together they laughed over it. She interested him in the American Civil War, and when she showed him a photo of Lincoln, he rearranged his pitch-black hair to look like the American president's. They had serious discussions, too, about art and literature, about life and death. Just as Gertrude believed that "Paris was the place that suited those of us that were to create the twentieth century art and literature," both she and Picasso felt strongly that they were to lead in this creation.

Gertrude and Leo Stein were becoming well known as arbiters of taste for the new art. Perhaps no one knew just who these strange Americans were, but the Saturday evening salon at the rue de Fleurus had become the most

Leo Stein.

stimulating meeting place for the creators of twentieth century art. Ideas and theories were argued passionately by all present, but the undisputed leader of the group was always Leo. He was brilliant and arrogant, and he did most of the talking. Yet all his talent and his impeccable taste seemed to come to nothing. He was unable to create or to produce. His fund of knowledge was enormous, as was his eagerness to show it off, but many of the guests grew restless in his presence. Only his loyal sister seemingly never tired of his lengthy diatribes on every conceivable subject.

Though Gertrude was immensely pleased at her position in the world of painting, she was even more anxious to continue her own work that could lead to the creation of a new literature. After she had finished and put aside her novel *QED*, she undertook the translation of three long short stories from the French—*Trois Contes*, by the nineteenth century writer Gustave Flaubert. She admired the Frenchman's precision, his character analysis and his sense of compositional balance. The translation was for her an exercise and a discipline, as well as a means of closely studying the process of creativity. When she had completed it, she was ready to begin work on three long stories of her own. They were called "The Good Anna," "The Gentle Lena," and "Melanchtha," and were to be collectively titled *Three Lives*. Each story is the history of a woman, two of them German immigrants, the simple and passive Lena, and the devoted, self-sacrificing Anna; the third is the complex and passionate mulatto Melanchtha.

These tales, especially "Melanchtha," are somewhat unconventional in language and style. Gertrude tried to re-create the actual sounds and rhythms of her characters, using colloquial speech and a kind of singsong repetition. Her overall desire was to create what she felt Cézanne had created in his paintings, works in which each element was as important as the entire work itself. Just as each human being is as important as another and a leaf is no less important than a tree, each moment in the life of her characters is of equal importance. The author herself never intrudes—the people in these stories speak for themselves, in their own voices.

Gertrude worked hard and steadily. Each evening at eleven o'clock, she would leave her visitors and go off to her room to write, usually until sunrise when she would go to bed and sleep until noon. She wrote first on endless scraps of paper, in pencil, later revising and copying it in ink, filling her brightly colored notebooks. She was meticulous and often another revision was necessary before she was completely satisfied.

In February 1906, *Three Lives* was completed, and she excitedly gave a copy of the manuscript to Sarah to read. Her sister-in-law was enthusiastic. But when Gertrude showed it to Leo, he showed little interest. He just didn't think his sister showed any promise of becoming a good writer.

Gertrude was hurt by Leo's reaction, but she was still determined to do what she could to have her book published. Before she could officially submit it, however, it had to be typed. There was a small portable typewriter in the house, but she didn't know how to use it. She was a writer and not a typist and was used to having menial work done for her. Fortunately, her old friend from Baltimore, Etta Cone, was in Paris, and she prevailed upon her to type the manuscript. When Miss Cone finished, *Three Lives* was submitted to publishers in America. The first one, Duffield and Company, found it too literary and unconventional and suggested an agent might be able to place parts of it in a magazine. An agent, Flora M. Holly, was found, but she had no success. With dogged determination, Gertrude turned it over to an old college friend, Mabel Weeks, but she too was unable to place Gertrude's work, though she tried such houses as Macmillan, Bobbs-Merrill, and the Open Court Publishing Company. The only solution seemed to be to have *Three Lives* published by a vanity press—that is, a publisher who publishes a book if the author undertakes to pay the costs. A house called Grafton Press in New York was chosen; they agreed to print one thousand copies at a cost of $660. But even though Frederick H. Hitchcock, the president of Grafton, was taking no risks in publishing the volume, he expressed horror at Gertrude's unusual style and strange use of language. An angry correspondence between publisher and author followed, the former writing to Gertrude that her grammar had to be corrected, among other things. Gertrude angrily rejected his suggestions, and he finally wrote her: "I think you have written a very peculiar book and it will be a hard thing to make people take it seriously."

However, Hitchcock had not given up. One day a

young American appeared at the rue de Fleurus to see Miss Gertrude Stein. He had come at the request of Hitchcock to find out if her English were poor or if she was merely an inexperienced writer. Gertrude, exasperated, laughed and told the young man to go ahead and print the book as written; the responsibility was all hers.

Shortly after completing *Three Lives*, Gertrude embarked on a far more ambitious project, one on which she worked exclusively for three years. It was to be a huge, all-encompassing work, the complete history of one family. However, as it developed it became a history of all human beings, the life of every possible sort of person who could live on this earth. More and more, Gertrude became silent during the Saturday evening gatherings in her home. Instead of speaking, she carefully observed all those around her, and when they had left she would make extensive charts and diagrams of each type of character and every possible kind of human reaction and experience.

In the summer of 1906, she and Leo went to Fiesole, a charming hilltop village overlooking the city of Florence. There Gertrude took long walks in the sun and spent hours reading in the city's English library, her mind always on plans for the new book. At night, she worked long hours on it, sure that what she was creating would be a masterpiece and would gain for her the glory she so needed. The style would be even more daring and original than that of *Three Lives*. Not only would each character be as important as the next, but each element that made up the personality of each person portrayed

Left to right: Gertrude, unidentified woman, Leo, a second unidentified woman, Michael, Allan, Sarah (*foreground*). Villa Bardi, Fiesole, summer 1905.

would be of equal importance. All of this would be expressed in a language that was fundamentally simple but structurally new and complex. The title of this extraordinary book would be *The Making of Americans*, and in the first chapter she explains her purpose in a language that is already her own:

The old people in a new world, the new people made out of the old, that is the story that I mean to tell, for that is what really is and what I really know.

Some of the fathers we must realise so that we can tell our story really, were little boys then, and they came across the water with their parents, the grandparents we need only just remember. Some of these our fathers and our mothers, were not even made then, and the women, the young mothers, our grandmothers we perhaps just have seen once, carried these our fathers and our mothers into the new world inside them, those women of the old world strong to bear them. Some looked very weak and little women, but even these so weak and little, were strong always, to bear many children.

These certain men and women, our grandfathers and grandmothers, with their children born and unborn with them, some whose children were gone ahead to prepare a home to give them all countries were full of women who brought with them many children; but only certain men and women and the children they had in them, to make many generations for them, will fill up this history for us of a family and its progress.

This history of an immigrant family, which becomes a history of all families, was not to be an ordinary one.

"Bear in mind," she warns the reader, "that this that I write down a little each day here on my scraps of paper for you is not just an ordinary kind of novel with a plot and conversations to amuse you, but a record of a decent family progress respectably lived by us and our fathers and our mothers, and our grandfathers, and grandmothers, and this is by me carefully a little each day to be written down here; and so my reader arm yourself in every kind of a way to be patient . . ."

The reader was, as a matter of fact, never patient, and *The Making of Americans* is one of the most widely known but least read books ever written. By the time Gertrude Stein finished it, it ran to more than half a million words—almost one thousand pages. The author had embarked on a highly original literary adventure, and, with this difficult, ambitious novel, took another step toward her goal of becoming "historical."

Chapter 5

GERTRUDE WAS HARD AT WORK ON HER NOVEL; IN ADDITION, SHE was adjusting to her new—and first—home in Paris. Her brother Leo was with her, and her older brother Michael and his wife Sarah lived a few blocks away. Everything seemed perfect when, on April 18, 1906, the Steins heard of the tremendous earthquake and fire that nearly destroyed the city of San Francisco. It was obviously essential that Michael and Sarah return there to see what had happened to their real estate holdings, which were the support of the entire family. Thus, as soon as arrangements for their passage could be made, they set off for the United States.

They brought with them several small paintings by Matisse, the first to be seen in America. They brought with them, too, wondrous tales of the beauties of Paris and the excitement of living there. Among their more fascinated listeners was a striking young woman with deepset eyes and shiny black hair, named Alice B. Toklas. She was twenty-eight years old, alert, intelligent, highspirited, and with a great interest in music. Her life in San Francisco was a comfortable one; she lived with and took care of her widowed father and her brother, had an interesting group of friends and a pleasant social life.

But the stories told to her by Michael and Sarah Stein made her feel that she should try for a different kind of life, and Paris seemed to be the place in which to try it. When she told her father that she might go off to Europe, he raised no serious objections since many young women were going abroad at the time. The only problem was finding the money for the trip, but that was solved a year later when Alice's grandfather died and left her enough money to travel to Europe.

In the fall of 1907, together with a friend named Harriet Levy, Alice arrived in Paris. On her first day there, she looked up the Steins and through them was invited to a party. There had been a series of parties for Michael and Sarah upon their return from America, during which they told tales of the United States just as they had previously recounted to San Franciscans their adventures in Paris. But this one party was to have special significance for it was there that Alice B. Toklas met Gertrude Stein.

Alice was immediately struck by Gertrude's powerful personality, by her deep resonant voice—and by a coral brooch she wore. An impulsive, romantic young woman, she heard a bell ring within her, she said, announcing the fact that she was in the presence of a genius. This happened to her only three times in her life: for Gertrude, for Picasso, and for the English philosopher Alfred North Whitehead. Most probably Gertrude heard no bell, but she was impressed by the lively young newcomer to Paris, a woman with an unmistakably aristocratic bearing as well as a strain of daring and wildness. The two found they had a great deal in common. They had each traveled in Europe as children and had both been brought up in San Francisco. Alice's mother had died when she was young, just as Gertrude's had. And to strengthen the enormous bond that was to grow between them, Gertrude needed someone to believe in her, and Alice needed someone in whom to believe. It was the beginning of the most important and lasting relationship in Gertrude's life.

During Alice's first months in Paris, Gertrude was her constant companion. They went to concerts together, to the theatre, and to the newly opened art galleries, where Alice was introduced to the works of the modern painters whose genius Gertrude had first recognized. Her eyes were being opened to a new world, and San Francisco was becoming more distant. The things she saw with Gertrude, the people she met—and above all Gertrude Stein herself—stimulated her and brought her to a way of life she had never thought possible.

Soon, too, Alice began to take on the role of Gertrude's secretary. Proofs of *Three Lives* were arriving from New York, and Alice read and corrected them. At the same time Gertrude was still hard at work on *The Making of Americans*, and the scraps of paper on which she wrote had to be transcribed into something readable. To help out, Alice learned to type in order to perform this task. She did so with enthusiasm—she believed that Gertrude was a great writer, and to help her in any way, even by typing her manuscript, was an honor.

The two women became inseparable. When in the summer of 1908 Leo and Gertrude decided to return to Fiesole for a few months, Alice and Harriet Levy joined them, renting a house nearby. Gertrude continued to work on *The Making of Americans*, with Alice faithfully typing the pieces as they were ready. During their spare time, they took trips together, Gertrude showing Alice the unique charms of smaller Italian towns like

49

Siena, Assisi, and Perugia, as well as the greatness and majesty of Rome.

At the end of the summer, Harriet Levy returned to Paris. Shortly thereafter, she cabled Alice to say that she had decided to return to San Francisco. For Alice this was a blow. Either she stayed alone in the little Paris apartment she had shared with Harriet or she joined her friend in returning to San Francisco. The idea of leaving Paris was almost unbearable, but so was the thought of living alone. It was Gertrude who found the ideal solution. With Leo's consent, though he doubted she would really fit in, she invited Alice B. Toklas to share with them the apartment at 27, rue de Fleurus.

Paris was more than ever bursting with creative energy at the time Alice B. Toklas moved into the Stein apartment, and many of the men and women who were generating that energy were frequent visitors to the rue de Fleurus. In 1907, a twenty-three-year-old German named Daniel-Henry Kahnweiler had come to Paris to open an art gallery. He was the first to show the works of the Cubists, thereby spreading their reputation. Picasso continued to come to the Stein salons as did Georges Braque, the cofounder of this revolutionary kind of painting. When she first met Picasso, Alice once again heard the bell in her head which heralded the appearance of a genius, just as she had upon meeting Gertrude. Another frequent visitor was Guillaume Apollinaire, the brilliant poet and art critic who was among the first to understand and appreciate what the Cubists were doing. Alice had a chance to meet Robert Delaunay, another Cubist; the

American painter Marsden Hartley; the Bulgarian Jules Pascin; and the influential and perceptive young collector from Germany, Wilhelm Uhde. Each of these men was little known at the time, but each was to take an important place in the history of twentieth century art. And each was somehow drawn to the heavy-set woman who presided over the evenings at the rue de Fleurus, who contributed more by carefully listening than did her nervous, agitated brother by talking.

Alice fit into this unusual household far more easily than Leo had ever expected. Somewhat timid in public, and far less vocal in her enthusiasms than Gertrude, she nonetheless enjoyed partaking of the atmosphere around her, so different from that of her San Francisco home. At a luncheon Gertrude gave for several painters, Alice laughed at Gertrude's idea of placing each artist opposite a painting of his own so as not to make one jealous of another. And she joined Gertrude and Leo at the famous banquet in honor of the primitive painter known as the Douanier Rousseau. It was on that occasion that the finest of Paris's young artists and writers climbed the hill to Picasso's studio to pay tribute to the elderly man who had been so shamefully ignored most of his life. It was modern art's homage to the simple values of the creative imagination.

Just as Alice began to share in the enjoyment of Gertrude's social life, she also assumed the duties of running the household. She did the shopping, she acted as receptionist, she planned the trips and handled Gertrude's correspondence. Increasingly she became an indispensable aid, allowing Gertrude to be free for her friends and, above all, for her work. And a deep love began to grow between the two women.

Gertrude, understandably, was disheartened by the reception accorded to *Three Lives* upon its publication in 1910. Few reviewers, outside of Baltimore, which considered her a hometown author, paid any attention to it. She sent a copy of the book to William James, but his response, though kind, was hardly encouraging. "You know how hard it is for me to read novels," he wrote to his former student. "Well, I read 30 or 40 pages and said, 'this is a fine new kind of realism—Gertrude Stein is great! I will go at it carefully when just the right mood comes.'" Presumably the right mood never did come, as there is no record of any further comment by James. A far more positive reaction came from the brilliant and controversial English writer H. G. Wells, who wrote Gertrude that he read the book "with deepening pleasure and admiration."

In spite of the lack of the acclaim she sought and felt she deserved, Gertrude continued to write with as much drive and energy as ever. She was aware of her difficulties in constructing an ordinary plot and, while completing *The Making of Americans*, she undertook to write a series of what she called "Portraits." Emphasizing the importance of characterization, these pieces would thereby not have to tell a story. At first she wrote about groups, such as "The Italians." She then sketched into words her friends, her acquaintances, almost everyone with whom she came into contact—beginning with Alice, who was the subject of a portrait called "Ada." But these portraits are far from ordinary ones, and almost all are extremely difficult to understand. The subject is generally not mentioned, nor does the reader find any recognizable characteristics of the subject. In a way, she was trying to do with words what Picasso and the Cubists did with plastic form and color—see every side of a subject, its every aspect, at the same time. The subject was thus seen by suggestion and not by literal representation. A relatively simple example of this complicated writing can be found in excerpts from her portrait of Picasso. This was, in fact, her first work to have mass circulation through publication in a magazine, as well as the first published writing on the artist.

One whom some were certainly following was one who was completely charming. One whom some were certainly following was one who was charming. One whom some were following was one who was completely charming. One whom some were following was one who was certainly charming.

Some were certainly following and were certain that the one they were then following was one working and was one bringing out of himself then something. Some were certainly following and were certain that the one they were then following was one bringing out of himself then something that was coming to be a heavy thing, a solid thing and a complete thing.

No one had written in this way before, and the response of most readers was one of shock. Accused of excessive use of repetition, Gertrude Stein replied that it was not repetition but recurrence that she employed, much as moviemakers did, since each image, each separate shot of a film, differs only minutely from the previous one. "I was doing what the cinema was doing," she wrote later, "I was making a continuous succession of the statement of what that person was until I had not many things but one thing."

These portraits, indecipherable to most readers, include some of Gertrude's best-known work. One is called "Miss Furr and Miss Skeene," and through the many repetitions, or recurrences, the reader comes to feel the desperation of the two women portrayed, as well as the monotony of their lives. Here her style is employed for an unmistakable effect. Another portrait, "Sacred Emily," contains the most famous line she ever wrote: "A rose is a rose is a rose is a rose."

These works, on which she labored with such determination, were unpublished. Gertrude Stein was known as a personality, a hostess, an art collector—but not as what she really was, a writer. With *Three Lives* published at her own expense and virtually ignored, the gigantic *The Making of Americans* completed and unpublished and unread, and an increasing number of portraits behind her, she decided in the spring of 1912 to vary her routine by going to Spain with Alice. She needed the change, a period in which to reflect on what she had done and what she would do.

The two women thoroughly enjoyed their visit to Spain, and the Spaniards evidently enjoyed their visitors just as much. They were a fascinating sight as they visited cathedrals and museums and hiked through picturesque mountain villages. Alice was invariably dressed in a black silk coat, with black gloves and a black hat; the only splash of color was found in the artificial flowers which seemed to grow out of her hat. Gertrude's costume was even more startling: each day she wore what seemed to be the same brown corduroy jacket and skirt, and on her head a small straw cap. Usually, too, she carried a cane. As 'the Spaniards watched this extraordinarily dressed woman march doggedly through their villages and towns, they were sure she must belong to some special religious order. Appropriately, the women were treated with great respect wherever they went.

Their first stop was the lovely old town of Avila, a completely walled medieval city, with eighty-six towers, a town which can be entered only through one of its nine gates. Alice was enchanted and felt she could stay there forever. For Gertrude, Avila had special meaning as it was the home of Saint Teresa, who had for a long time been one of her heroines. It was no wonder that Gertrude felt close to this energetic woman who had reformed the Carmelite order, founded small convents and monasteries throughout Spain and was known for her friendliness, humor, and compassionate understanding. Saint Teresa's love of laughter, charm, and unwavering determination in the face of all odds were indeed qualities with which Gertrude Stein could identify.

From Avila, they moved on to the great capital of Madrid, where Gertrude took Alice to her first bullfight, which she liked somewhat more than she thought she would, and where they were both delighted by the well-known Spanish dancer Argentina, whom they watched perform night after night. Gertrude was inspired to write three poems, as a result of her experiences in Spain—"Susie Asado," "Preciosilla," and "Gypsies in Spain." The first two are said to be attempts at reproducing the rhythm of flamenco dancing in words.

After Madrid came Granada, the site of the fabulous Alhambra, the fourteenth century palace of the Moorish kings. There Gertrude decided to work seriously again. Night after night, in her room at the Washington Irving Hotel, she applied what she had already learned to something new. In her portraits, she had abandoned plot and concentrated on characterization alone. Now she would write not of people, but of nature and of objects. She set out to express color and movement, "to express things seen not as one knows them but as they are when one sees them without remembering having looked at them." These would be still lifes in prose, patterns of assorted words, compositions of unidentifiable fragments. The results of this experiment were collected under the title *Tender Buttons*. Once again, Gertrude Stein had broken new ground, but once again she had written a work that would remain a mystery to most readers.

The volume is divided into three sections: one is called "Objects," another is called "Food," and the third, "Rooms." "Objects" includes "A Box," "Mildred's Umbrella," and "More." Under the title "A Petticoat," Gertrude Stein wrote: "A light white, a disgrace, an ink spot, a rosy charm."

Among the items included in "Food" are "Roastbeef," "Breakfast," "Cups," and "Orange In." There are four brief sections called "Chicken." One of them reads: "Alas a dirty word, alas a dirty third alas a dirty third, alas a dirty bird."

"Rooms" is a single, longer piece, as difficult to decipher as the short examples above. These *Tender Buttons* are obviously experimental; in them the author was not so much interested in what the reader thought, but in solving her own linguistic and literary problems. For one, she wanted to eliminate naming the objects described— which she was able to do in many of these pieces. In explanation, she later wrote:

Was there not a way of naming things that would not invent names, but mean names without naming them. . . .

I had always been very impressed from the time that I was very young by having had it told me and then afterwards feeling it myself that Shakespeare in the forest of Arden had created a forest without mentioning the things that make a forest. You feel it all but he does not name its names.

Satisfied with her writing, pleased with the happy days she had spent in Spain, Gertrude returned to Paris in surprisingly bad spirits. A restlessness had come over her, so she welcomed and accepted an invitation that awaited her to visit the Villa Curonia, the home of Mabel Dodge, located in the small village of Arcetri near Florence.

"A stoutish woman with a very sturdy fringe of heavy hair over her forehead, heavy long lashes and very pretty

eyes with a very old-fashioned coquetry" was the way
Gertrude described the hostess who greeted her and Alice
at the Villa Curonia that fall. In Mabel Dodge, whom she
had met through a mutual friend not long before, she
clearly recognized a kindred spirit, for Mrs. Dodge was
still another strong, magnetic, and independent woman.
A wealthy American patron of the arts, it seemed that a
salon followed her wherever she went throughout her
lifetime—from Buffalo to Florence, to Philadelphia, and
finally to Taos, New Mexico. She attached herself to writers everywhere, writers as different as Gertrude Stein
and D. H. Lawrence. She was forever seeking to lead the
avant-garde and had remarkable success in doing so.
After reading the manuscript of *The Making of Americans*, she was overwhelmed: "One of the most remarkable things I have ever read," she wrote the author. Thus
began a fine friendship: Mabel Dodge had found a writer
whose cause she could champion, and Gertrude had met
a woman who sincerely admired her and appreciated
what she was doing.

Gertrude's stay at the Villa Curonia was pleasant, from
the day of her arrival. That day, according to her hostess,
she was wearing "a sort of kimono made of brown corduroy." But it was hot as it can sometimes be in the Tuscan
autumn, "and when she sat down, fanning herself with
her broad-brimmed hat with its wilted dark-brown rib-
bon, she exhaled a vivid steam all around her. When she
got up she frankly used to pull her clothes off from where
they had stuck to her great legs. Yet with all this she was
not at all repulsive. On the contrary, she was positively,

richly attractive in her grand *ampleur*. She always seemed to like her own fat anyway, and that helps other people to accept it. She had none of the funny embarrassments Anglo-Saxons have about the flesh. She gloried in hers."

The two women got along beautifully, though Mabel Dodge did not share Gertrude's enthusiasm for Alice, whom she found dull. Alice, for her part, seemed annoyed at Gertrude's enthusiasm for Mrs. Dodge and what she called her "Buffalo sort of vulgarity." Yet the animosity between Alice and Mabel Dodge did not diminish the latter's great respect for Gertrude's literary talent nor for her powerful personality and her "laugh like a beefsteak." One evening, she wrote in her memoirs, Gertrude "sent me such a strong look over the table that it seemed to cut across the air to me in a band of electrified steel—a smile traveling across on it—powerful—Heavens!"

During the daytime, Gertrude and Alice walked briskly through the lovely countryside surrounding Florence, rediscovering parts of the country that Gertrude had already become acquainted with in the past. In the evenings, there were visitors—everyone always came to Mabel Dodge's, wherever it was. Gertrude met André Gide, the great French writer, who didn't interest her, as well as the well-known actress Muriel Draper. She also met a strange woman named Constance Fletcher, who at a young age had written the tremendous best seller *Kismet* under the pseudonym of George Fleming (a respectable woman could not be acknowledged as the author of such a romantic work at the time).

At night, she worked by candlelight, in the study of

Mabel's husband (she was to have four of them) who was away on a visit to America. Painstakingly, oblivious of what might be taking place around her, she composed a portrait of Constance Fletcher and one of "Mabel Dodge at the Villa Curonia." Each night she would scribble four or five lines on a scrap of paper, to be typed by Alice the following day.

When Gertrude and Alice were ready to return to Paris, Mabel Dodge was shown her portrait. She was delighted, so much so that she had three hundred copies of it privately printed for her friends and thus help to spread the fame of Gertrude Stein. Reactions to it, however, were mixed. "The days are wonderful and the nights are wonderful and life is pleasant" was the simple beginning of this portrait, but it then went on in Gertrude's complex and often confusing style. "How do you know that it is a portrait of you, after all?" the American poet Edwin Arlington Robinson asked Mabel Dodge. The distinguished English novelist, playwright, and ardent Zionist Israel Zangwill seemed hurt when he read it: "And I always thought she was such a healthy-minded young woman, what a terrible blow it must be for her poor dear brother, " he wrote.

The blow to Gertrude's "poor dear brother" was not a serious or unexpected one. It was further evidence that his sister had absolutely no talent, and he had slowly been losing all interest in her. As for the portrait of Mabel Dodge, it was for him "damned nonsense." "A portrait of a person that I know pretty intimately which conveys absolutely nothing to me, a far from inexperienced reader with no prejudices in the matter, seems to me to have something the matter with it. (I've tried to read the darned thing a number of times.)" In the same letter to a friend, written from Paris, Leo couples his contempt for Gertrude's work with his disapproval of Picasso's development as a Cubist: "Both he and Gertrude are using their intellects, which they ain't got, to do what would need the finest critical tact, which they ain't got neither, and they are in my belief turning out the most Godalmighty rubbish that is to be found."

When Gertrude returned to the apartment at the rue de Fleurus, Leo was gone. The break between them was complete, and it was just a matter of time before it would become formal. Over the past few years, an indifference had grown between them. There were no fights and no drama, merely a gradual separation. The reasons are difficult to understand, but Leo's disregard for his sister's work certainly contributed to it. Throughout her lifetime, Gertrude needed praise and encouragement, needed to surround herself with people who believed in what she was doing. Leo was not one of those, and as Gertrude's personality developed and she acquired her own circle of friends and admirers, she was no longer dependent on her brother. Alice supplied her with the love and confidence she needed, and Alice too was there to take over the responsibility of head of the household for practical matters. Leo, with his constant talking and fits of depression and nervousness, got in his sister's way, while Alice replaced him by quietly going about the business of taking care of Gertrude's personal comfort. Before Gertrude,

Alice B. Toklas felt she was in the presence of genius; Leo was sure that he was not. It was an impossible situation that had developed between brother and sister, and it was in the interest of both that they separate.

At the time of their estrangement, Leo wrote: "There is practically nothing we don't either disagree about, or at least regard with different sympathies." And Gertrude later wrote that "Leo continued to believe in what he was saying when he was arguing and I began not to find it interesting."

Lack of mutual interest—this seems to be the real cause of the break between a brother and sister who had once been so close. In a short time Leo moved to Florence with the woman he would eventually marry. The valuable collection of paintings was divided without enmity between brother and sister, by correspondence. "I hope that we will all live happily ever after and maintain our respective and due proportions while sucking gleefully our respective oranges," Leo wrote at the end. Two sensitive, intelligent people seem to have realized that their relationship, once so close, was over. Rather than settle for a more superficial friendship, they parted once and for all.

Chapter 6

IN 1913, GERTRUDE STEIN WAS BUT ONE YEAR FROM HER FOR-
tieth birthday. She had worked hard, and steadily, for
many years, and the result was thousands of pages of
manuscript—almost all of them unpublished. The process
of creating is important and satisfying to a writer, yet for
most writers, and certainly for Gertrude, publication and
consequent praise is also essential. She admitted that she
despaired from time to time and would become depressed
about every three months. But how could she find a publisher?

In January of 1913, she and Alice went to England in
search of one. Gertrude had had word that John Lane, a
respected and courageous London publisher, might be the
right man to publish her books. She contacted Lane, and
they became friends. Through him she met many of England's most important intellectuals of the period. They
had all heard of her—of her collection of paintings, her
charm and intelligence, even her eccentric wardrobe. But
very few knew her writing. John Lane's wife, an American from Boston, did read *Three Lives*, however, and was
enthusiastic. She advised her husband to publish it, but
Lane said he needed time to think it over and suggested
that Gertrude return to London in July.

So Gertrude returned to Paris, once again disappointed
at not having found someone to publish her work. Nonetheless, as her circle of acquaintances widened, her fame
spread, and her magnetic charm drew more and more
people to the rue de Fleurus.

By now, they came from all over, even if they didn't
quite understand who this much-spoken-of woman was.

Studio of Leo and Gertrude Stein, 27, rue de Fleurus, about 1913.

Top row, left to right: MATISSE *Joy of Life;* VALLOTTON *Reclining Nude;* PICASSO *Seated Nude;* PICASSO *Woman with a Fan. Middle row:* MATISSE *Olive Trees;* PICASSO *The Reservoir, Horta;* PICASSO *Still Life;* PICASSO *Houses on a Hill, Horta;* PICASSO *Landscape;* PICASSO *Young Girl with a Basket of Flowers. Bottom row:* 3 watercolors by Cézanne; PICASSO *Head of a Young Man;* 2 obscured works, and an unidentified painting.

Studio of Leo and Gertrude Stein, 27, rue de Fleurus, about 1913.

Top row, left to right: MATISSE *Music (Study)*; PICASSO *Seated Woman in a Hood*; PICASSO *Young Acrobat on a Ball*; PICASSO *Standing Female Nude. Second row:* MANGUIN *Standing Nude*; PICASSO *Two Women at a Bar. Third row:* DAUMIER *Head of an Old Woman*; PICASSO *Still Life with Glasses and Fruit*; PICASSO *Portrait of Gertrude Stein*; PICASSO *Study for Nude with Drapery*; PICASSO *Violin*; PICASSO *The Little Glass*; CEZANNE *Portrait of Mme Cézanne*; CEZANNE *Landscape with Spring House. Fourth row:* RENOIR *Brunette*; MANET *Ball Scene*; CEZANNE *Man with a Pipe*; PICASSO *Still Life with Fruit and Glass*; CEZANNE *Bathers. Bottom row:* Unidentified paintings and drawings, among them 4 Cézanne watercolors.

They came to look and to listen and to see who was there —complete strangers from Germany, Hungary, and Romania, odd members of royalty with dubious titles. From England came a more serious group, many of whom Gertrude had met on her visit there. Among them were two American-born Englishmen, the sculptor Jacob Epstein and the controversial painter-essayist-novelist Wyndham Lewis, who later turned violently against modern art and literature. Another frequent visitor was Roger Fry, a brilliant art critic who had for a few years been curator of paintings of New York's Metropolitan Museum of Art and at whose country home in England Gertrude and Alice had stayed. Through Fry she met Clive Bell, a leader of London's influential Bloomsbury group, as well as the famed portraitist Augustus John. The leaders of the newly formed Futurist group, Severini and Marinetti, too, came to Gertrude's salon, but she found them—and their art— dull. Then there were many Americans, as diverse as the stage designer Robert Edmond Jones and the Harvard-educated revolutionary John Reed. Most important there were two American writers who would champion Gertrude's literary cause. One was Henry McBride, a writer for the newspaper, the New York *Sun*. The other was Carl Van Vechten, a novelist and critic who was to become Gertrude's close friend for life.

Mabel Dodge had sent a copy of her portrait to Van Vechten; the latter was so enthusiastic that he sought out and profoundly admired *Three Lives*. He then read the "Portraits" of Picasso and Matisse which had been published in *Camera Work* in 1912. He was convinced that

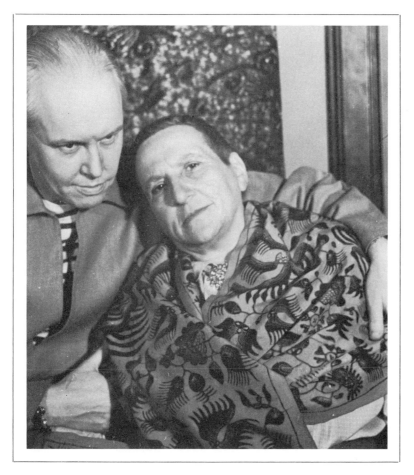

Carl Van Vechten and Gertrude Stein.

the author of all these works was a genius.

Mabel Dodge, on her return to America, did all she could to spread and make known the fame of Gertrude Stein. The timing was perfect, for New York was in the midst of a cultural and artistic uproar. It had all started with the Armory Show, an art exhibition which opened February 13, 1913, at the Sixty-ninth Regiment Armory. Eleven hundred works of modern art were displayed, giving Americans their first opportunity to see what had been done in Europe since the time of the Postimpressionists. Every recent trend in European art was represented, from the Fauvism of Matisse, Vlaminck, and Derain, the Cubism of Picasso and Braque, to the futurism of Severini and the abstract art of Kandinsky. The sensation of the exhibit was Marcel Duchamp's *Nude Descending a Staircase*, a painting which shocked critics and public alike.

But the entire exhibition was a shock, the object of wild attacks by the press and scorn by the public. Yet it stirred up interest in modern art that was to increase throughout the United States in the years to come.

At the center of this storm was Mabel Dodge, fighting valiantly for the cause of modern art and doing her best to identify Gertrude Stein with this struggle. The paintings that offended the public sensibility were bound to be recognized in the end; and the same was true for the literature of Gertrude Stein.

Mrs. Dodge's opportunity to promote Gertrude's work, as well as herself, came when she was asked to write an article for a magazine called *Arts and Decoration*. The subject she chose was Gertrude Stein and her "Portrait of Mabel Dodge at the Villa Curonia." The article was effusive in its praise of Gertrude:

In a large studio in Paris, hung with paintings by Renoir, Matisse and Picasso, Gertrude Stein is impelling language to induce new states of consciousness, and in doing so language becomes with her a creative art rather than a mirror of history . . . Many roads are being broken— what a wonderful word—"broken"! and out of the shattering and the petrification of today—up from the cleavage and disintegration—we will see order emerging tomorrow. Is it so difficult to remember that life at birth is always painful and rarely lovely? How strange it is to think that the rough-hewn trail of today will become tomorrow the path of least resistance, over which the average will drift with all the ease and serenity of custom. All the labor of evolution is condensed into this one fact, of the vitality of the individual making way for the many. We can but praise the high courage of the road breakers, admitting as we infallibly must, in Gertrude Stein's own words, and with true Bergsonian faith—"something is certainly coming out of them."

Gertrude was thrilled with the article. "I am proud as punch," she wrote Mabel Dodge. "Do send me a half a dozen copies of it. I want to show it to everybody. *Hurrah for gloire.*" Glory had not yet arrived, but Gertrude Stein felt more than ever that it was coming.

Another sign that she was on her way came in the summer of 1914 when John Lane let her know that he was ready to draw up the contract for the publication of *Three Lives* and discuss publication of other of her books. Hastily they prepared for their trip, and on July 5, Gertrude and Alice arrived in London.

John Lane, too, held a salon, each Sunday afternoon, and soon after their arrival the two women attended it, full of expectations and in high spirits. But the talk that afternoon was disconcerting; instead of discussing literature, the other guests talked of war, for the most part agreeing that it was a matter of days before the entire continent of Europe would be involved in a huge conflict. This was certainly not news to Gertrude, but it was a fact that she refused to recognize because she didn't want to. War was unthinkable.

At the end of the afternoon, she and John Lane tried to set up a mutually convenient appointment; because of the publisher's other commitments, they found it necessary to put off the formal contract discussions for a few weeks.

So Gertrude and Alice had time to enjoy themselves in London and in the countryside surrounding the capital. As always, they were a strange sight, whether walking briskly through the streets of London or rambling idly through the country. For this trip to England, Gertrude's costume consisted of a short corduroy skirt, a white silk shirt, a small hat on her head, and the usual sandals on her feet. Alice's costume this time was somewhat Oriental; from her ears hung huge earrings, from her arms bracelets, and around her neck, heavy chains. Gertrude frankly admitted that she wanted to call attention to herself, and she most certainly did.

But it wasn't only her costume that impressed the people she met; it was also her keen intelligence, her ability to listen and observe and then respond perceptively. She met more of England's great literary figures, among them A. E. Housman, the poet. But most important, she met the mathematician and philosopher Alfred North Whitehead (an occasion on which Alice heard the bells of genius ring a third, and last, time). Gertrude, Alice, Alfred North Whitehead, and his wife got along beautifully, and at once. On Friday, she would sign the contract with Lane for *Three Lives* but he would wait to see how it was received before planning publication of the other books. After the signing, Gertrude and Alice would go to the Whiteheads' home in the country, at Lockridge, for the weekend before returning to Paris.

Triumphantly, her first contract in hand, Gertrude set out for Lockridge. Once there, however, it was clear that it was not time for celebration. War had come and was spreading. On August 3, Germany invaded Belgium and declared war on France. The following day, Great Britain declared war on Germany. World War I had started, France itself was threatened by a German invasion, and there was no possibility of Gertrude and Alice returning to their home. The Whiteheads graciously prevailed upon the two women to stay with them at Lockridge until it was safe to return to Paris.

Gertrude was depressed. She felt displaced, she worried about France and Paris and her home and the piles of manuscripts she had left behind. Whitehead's company was a great consolation. The two shared a love of walking through the fields and would do so together for hours, finding vast areas of common interest as they discussed philosophy and history and literature. But the news from France was bad, very bad. The threat to Paris was so great that on September 1 the French government moved its headquarters from Paris to Bordeaux. The thought of Paris being overrun and ruled by Germans appalled Gertrude, who as a result spent more and more time closed up in her room in a state of depression. The fierce battle of the Marne broke out, and the French army resisted the German advance valiantly. On September 9, when they could already see the Eiffel Tower in the distance, the Germany army was miraculously turned back. Their orders were to retreat.

Paris was saved. When Alice ran to Gertrude's room with the news, Gertrude could hardly believe it; and when she did, she burst into tears of relief. Now all her attention was turned to making plans for the trip back to Paris. The Whiteheads continued to entertain, and at their home Gertrude talked with Lytton Strachey and Bertrand Russell, two of England's most important intellectual figures. But that didn't matter; what mattered most was returning home to her work, her manuscripts, her city, her world.

On October 15, Gertrude and Alice were once again in Paris, but the city that greeted them was far different from the one they had left. Mobilization and war had broken up the groups that had founded modern art and literature. Most Frenchmen had been drafted; many of the foreigners had joined the Foreign Legion. Braque, Derain, and Apollinaire were in the army—Apollinaire having taken out French citizenship in order to join. Because the front was relatively close to Paris, they were able to come to the capital on leave, but it wasn't the same. Art and literature had come to a standstill. Only Picasso remained a nonparticipant, believing that war was business for soldiers. But he too was depressed, as he watched Eva, the woman who had replaced Fernande in his life, dying of a slow, painful illness.

In addition, it was a time of material hardship. All the gaiety had left Paris; half the city seemed to have disappeared, the other half was afflicted with nightly blackouts, food shortages, and fear. Gertrude was unable to work. Her new friend Carl Van Vechten was trying desperately to sell her pieces in America but was having little success. *Tender Buttons* was published in the States in an edition of one thousand copies by a new firm, named Claire–Marie, but there was little critical response. The name of Gertrude Stein was becoming known, but largely as an object of ridicule. Money, too, was short and the wartime cost of living high, so much so that Gertrude was forced to sell her last Matisse to her brother Michael. By springtime, frightened by the increasing number of bombing alerts and absolutely terrified by the Zeppelin raids over Paris, Gertrude and Alice left France.

One of the few places in Europe which was safe from the war was Spain, so the two women decided to go to the island of Mallorca for the summer. Today a center for American and British expatriates as well as a major tourist attraction, Mallorca was at that time a quiet, peaceful spot, and Alice and Gertrude found a pleasant house near the town of Palma. The landscape was beautiful, the climate mild, fruits and vegetables plentiful. Gertrude was again able to write, to take walks in the country, to regain the calm she had lost during the difficult months in Paris. By the time the summer ended, news from Paris was still bad, so the return home was postponed. It was a period of waiting—made pleasant by the surroundings in which she found herself. Nonetheless, Gertrude did manage to work, starting on a series of "Plays," as she called them. They were inspired by the suggestive Spanish landscape, and to her there existed a fundamental connection between a landscape and a play. "A landscape is such a natural arrangement for a battlefield or a play that one must write plays," she explained. Her plays, however, bear no relation to what we think of as plays. Drama, above all, is missing, and these plays seem more like extensions of her portraits—with the addition of the character's voice.

By the summer of 1916, things began to look better for France and for the outcome of the war, so Gertrude and Alice returned to Paris. The city had changed: it was far less gloomy than it had been, and there was an air of cheerful optimism. Still the war was far from over, and the time had come for Gertrude and Alice to become involved in it. The question was how, and the answer was supplied when they spotted a car with a sign on it reading "American Fund for French Wounded." The driver, an American girl, told them where the headquarters of the organization could be found and off they went to offer their services. Their offer was gratefully accepted, on the condition that they had means of transportation. This was a problem; Gertrude had no car, nor could she have driven one if she had. But with her usual determination she convinced some New York cousins to raise the money to buy a car and have it shipped to France. She herself took driving lessons in an old taxicab from a friend she had known in Mallorca.

When the car, a Ford, arrived, she was ready for it. It was converted into a truck and, with a bottle of white wine, swiftly christened "Auntie," after Gertrude's Aunt Pauline "who always behaved admirably in emergencies and behaved fairly well most times if she was properly flattered." Auntie did behave well most of the time, but it is doubtful that she was properly flattered for Gertrude knew very little about cars—most important, she had never mastered the art of going into reverse. One incident followed another during Auntie's service, but the Ford's driver was uncannily able to get help in even the most difficult situations. The sight of a dumpy, eccentrically dressed and obviously helpless woman at the wheel moved Frenchmen to do their best to come to her aid. The woman with the helmet-shaped hat on her head, body covered with a uniformlike coat, and sandals on her feet was clearly irresistible.

Gertrude and Alice's first assignment was to open up a supply depot in Perpignan, in the south of France near the Spanish border. From there they were to deliver supplies personally to surrounding hospitals. The trip south was not free of incidents with Auntie, but Gertrude always managed to get help, often from the soldiers she inevitably picked up on the way. She liked these young men, she liked to listen to the stories of their lives and families, and they in turn responded to her genuine interest. The same was true in Perpignan, where Gertrude ably and sympathetically dealt with the men with whom she came into contact. Alice took care of the office work and the bookkeeping, while Gertrude, in delivering sup-

Gertrude Stein and Alice B. Toklas, 1917.

plies to hospitals and packages to wounded soldiers, also supplied a maternal warmth and good cheer.

When their job in Perpignan was completed, the two women returned to Paris where they were reassigned to the town of Nîmes to do the same work they had done in Perpignan. By this time, the United States had entered the war, and more and more they came into contact with the American army. Gertrude was delighted to hear her own language spoken once again, and endlessly questioned the soldiers she met about their lives in America. She liked them and felt for them, and they in turn warmed up easily to her charms. Few, if any, knew who she was; to them she was merely a kindly, lively woman with a beguiling laugh and a spirited sense of humor.

Gertrude was, of course, able to write little during the course of the war. However, a few articles were published in New York which did increase her reading public. One was called "Have They Attacked Mary. He Giggled," an amusing piece published in the popular magazine *Vanity Fair*. The other articles were published as a result of her own response to a series of parodies of her work which were published in the *Life* magazine of that time. Not terribly amused by the pieces by Kenneth Roberts that made fun of her, she wrote to the editor suggesting that the writer parodied was more original and more amusing than the man who was making fun of her. To her surprise the editor of *Life* responded positively to her suggestion. As a result, *Life* published a poem called "Woodrow Wilson" and an article entitled "Relief Work in France."

In November 1918, the war came to an end, and an armistice was signed. After a brief assignment in Alsace where they aided in the rehabilitation of refugees, Alice and Gertrude returned to Paris. Life could, they hoped, pick up where they had left it more than four years before.

Chapter 7

THE PARIS TO WHICH GERTRUDE STEIN RETURNED AT THE END of World War I was not the same as the one she had left, and her life there was to differ considerably during the 1920s from the one she had led before. She was no longer at the center of a group of crusading artists: Fauvism and Cubism had been accepted by the public, and their creators were no longer frequent visitors to the Stein salon. Apollinaire, the voice of the new art, was dead as a result of injuries suffered during the war. Matisse was in Nice and seldom visited Paris. Even Picasso no longer came to see Gertrude for a while. The two friends had argued over what Gertrude called "nothing at all" and did not see each other for a short period. Gertrude Stein, the leader of the avant-garde, the young convention-breaking writer who drew inspiration from and gave support to the pioneering French artists, had been transformed into Gertrude Stein, a wise, middle-aged woman whose visitors were largely the young writers who had come to Paris from America. It was a new generation, one she herself called the Lost Generation.

Americans had, for the most part, been uninvolved with Europe prior to the First World War. Travel had been expensive and difficult, and knowledge of the Old World had come from books. But with America's entry into the European war, thousands of young Americans had their first look at this Old World. For some the war was an adventure, and for many the contact with another culture was stimulating; but when the war ended and the men who had come to maturity during it returned home, they felt somehow lost and rootless. At a time when they should have been choosing their professions, they had been fighting useless battles in foreign lands. Many of the artists and writers among them felt a special personal emptiness when trying to begin their lives again. They came to feel that their own country was culturally barren, and their personal dissatisfaction led them to believe that everything was better in Europe. For this reason, many of them returned there after the war, in search of new values, to write their novels, to find the romance and creative excitement that was lacking at home.

They went everywhere in Europe, but most of the writers were drawn to Paris as the center of literary activity. They drifted to the wide boulevard Montparnasse and sat for hours at the cafés that lined it—the Dôme and the Select and the Coupole. They talked of the books they would write, the poems they would pen, and the paintings they would put on canvas. And some of them actually did more than talk of their plans.

Many of these "lost" young men came to Paris armed with two addresses, that of a small bookshop on the rue de l'Odéon and that of Gertrude Stein. The bookshop was called Shakespeare and Company, and it had been founded by a young American woman named Sylvia Beach, who had come to settle in Paris in 1917. It was not an ordinary bookstore: Shakespeare and Company specialized in English-language books, not the best sellers but the experimental works of the younger writers. It was crowded with tables and shelves of books, and its walls were lined with photos of distinguished authors. It was a place where one could come to read or to talk, where writers could come to make contact with other writers. It was warmed in winter by a huge stove and at all times by its cheerful owner. "Sylvia had a lively, sharply sculptured face," Ernest Hemingway wrote, "brown eyes that were as alive as a small animal's and gay as a young girl's, and wavy brown hair that was brushed back from her fine forehead and cut thick below her ears and at the line of the collar of the brown velvet jacket she wore. She had pretty legs and she was kind, cheerful and interested, and loved to make jokes and gossip. No one that I ever knew was nicer to me."

Shortly after Sylvia Beach opened her shop, she was visited by two rather unusual-looking American women. "One of them," she wrote, "with a very fine face, was stout, wore a long robe and on her head a most becoming top of a basket. She was accompanied by a slim, dark, whimsical woman; she reminded me of a gypsy." The women were, of course, Gertrude and Alice, and they were enthusiastic about the new store and its owner. When Sylvia decided to open a lending library service, Gertrude was its first subscriber. Not only that, she composed an advertisement that was sent out to other potential subscribers: "Rich and Poor in English to Subscribers in French and Other Latin Tongues," which was followed by a statement of the book rental terms.

Just as American writers found themselves going to Shakespeare and Company, they also found their way to 27, rue de Fleurus. Very few had read Gertrude's writings, but all had heard of her collection of paintings and all had heard stories of her passion for literature, her warmth, and her genuine interest in people. Their reception depended very much upon their hostess's immediate reaction to them. Gertrude could be as cold as she could be warm, as unfriendly as she could be friendly, but these members of the Lost Generation nonetheless sought refuge, as the critic Van Wyck Brooks wrote, "in the mature Gertrudian bosom, much like that of their faraway prairie mothers, but of a most gratifying sophistication. Miss Stein gave them back their nursery rhymes and they had fine, babbling times together."

The large, motherly woman with the infectious laugh and quick wit was, it is true, singularly American, yet combined with her Americanism there was the culture accumulated in Europe during the first two decades of the twentieth century. So it seemed only natural for these lost young men to come to her and seek her often perceptive advice.

Among them were some who would eventually be among the major writers of their age. She encouraged them and made them feel that what they were doing was important. Sometimes, the reverse was true, as in the case of Sherwood Anderson. Anderson was not a young man —he was only two years younger than Gertrude—but he was a new writer. A respectable Ohio businessman with a wife and children, he had suffered a nervous breakdown in his late thirties, after which he left his job and family and went off to Chicago to write his first novel. This was not published until he was forty years old. In 1921, he visited Paris, and shortly after his arrival he went to Shakespeare and Company to ask Sylvia Beach to introduce him to Gertrude Stein. Sylvia took him there: from the moment they met, there was no doubt that it was the beginning of a long and devoted friendship. Gertrude had many profound relationships with many friends throughout her lifetime, yet she was also known to quarrel with and completely terminate relationships with people to whom she had once been close. But she and Anderson remained loyal to one another until the latter's death. He was immediately enchanted: "Imagine a strong woman with legs like stone pillars sitting in a room hung with Picassos. The woman is the very symbol of health and strength. She laughs. She smokes cigarettes. She tells stories with an American shrewdness in getting the tang and the kick into the telling." He was no less impressed with her writing and never hesitated to tell her how influential her works had been to his own development. It was from her that he had learned the importance of words and the absolute necessity of solid craftsmanship. "Miss Stein is a worker in words with the same loving touch in her strong fingers that was characteristic of the women of the kitchens of the old brick houses in the town of my boyhood," he wrote. "She is an American woman of the old sort, one who cares for the hand-made goodies and scorns the factory-made foods, and in her own great kitchen she is making something with her materials, something sweet to the tongue and fragrant to the nostrils."

The praise and devotion Gertrude received from the author of *Winesburg, Ohio* came at an especially opportune moment since a feeling of discouragement had inevitably accompanied her difficulties in getting her writ-

Sherwood Anderson.

ings published. "I don't think you quite realize," she wrote to Anderson, "what it meant to have someone and you have been the only one quite simply to understand what it is all about simply understand as any one would suppose everyone would understand and to so charmingly and directly tell it to me."

The mutual affection and respect they felt for each other never failed; the two writers praised each other in public at every opportunity. Such, unfortunately, was not the case with Ernest Hemingway, whose name has been most closely associated with Gertrude's. Theirs was a close and intense friendship, which nonetheless was to end bitterly, without any specific reason.

Hemingway was born in 1899 and by the time he was nineteen years old he was a cub reporter for the Kansas City *Star*. A young man craving adventure and excitement, he volunteered his services as an ambulance driver during the First World War. He was seriously wounded and almost lost his life on the Italian front. In 1919, he went to Toronto where he wrote feature stories for the *Star Weekly*, and in 1921 he was back in Europe, with a new wife. In 1922, when he came to Paris, he had with him a letter of introduction from Sherwood Anderson to Gertrude Stein.

Gertrude was immediately won over by the large young man, with deep black hair, dark intense eyes, and a small mustache. She found his eyes to be "passionately interested rather than interesting." As he entered her studio, dressed in his usual patched coat and sneakers, she was struck by the self-assurance that lay behind his warm Mid-

Ernest Hemingway.

western grin. Hemingway reciprocated and was charmed by his hostess's strength of personality. They established an immediate rapport, and at their first meeting the young journalist urged Gertrude and Alice to dine with him and his wife at their apartment. They did so, and Gertrude spent most of the evening poring over Hemingway's manuscripts. Some she liked, and some she didn't, but she recognized an unmistakable talent. Hemingway listened attentively and appreciatively that first evening and later, during their long walks through Paris's Left Bank. His work soon reflected Gertrude's advice and the influence of her own writing more directly than had any other writer's. The two became intimate friends, and Hemingway shared all his problems—personal as well as professional—with the older woman. As time went on, he increasingly took advantage of the warmth and comfort and good food offered at the rue de Fleurus.

He had problems. His wife was pregnant, which meant he would have to lead a somewhat more settled life and he would need money. The only means he had of earning money was by continuing with his journalism; but that in turn took so much time that he was unable to concentrate on his creative writing which he preferred. Gertrude sympathized thoroughly and feared that the journalist might indeed kill the creative artist. Her advice was to return to Toronto and to work hard and steadily on his journalism so that he might accumulate enough money to return to Europe and devote full time to his more serious writing.

Hemingway took her advice, and when he returned to Europe, it was with a newborn son for whom Gertrude and Alice were godmothers. The friendship picked up where it had left off. The young writer needed Gertrude's help and approval, which she unfailingly gave to him. And, for his part, he encouraged her, saying that *The Making of Americans* was "the best stuff I have ever read," and did his best to find an American publisher for it. He did, in fact, find a magazine willing to publish excerpts, and he himself copied portions of the one existing manuscript toward that end.

However, this seemingly indestructible, mutually beneficial friendship came to an end in the mid-1920s. The specific reasons for the break between these two once-solid friends remain unclear, but it seems to have begun when Hemingway quarreled with Sherwood Anderson, and Gertrude sided with Anderson. From that time on, Hemingway and Gertrude appear to have drifted apart, possibly because they no longer needed each other. During the first years of their friendship, Hemingway acknowledged to one and all his great debt to Gertrude, both as a friend and as a literary mentor. But by the time *The Sun Also Rises* was published in 1926, Hemingway was so commercially successful that he forgot, publicly at least, how much he had learned from his friend and how much she had helped him. They saw each other less and less frequently, and Gertrude demonstrated once more her ability to forget even the existence of people who had not lived up to her expectations. Once they met on a street and Hemingway told her he was rich and old and tired and wanted to resume their friendship, but Gertrude replied that she was none of those things and preferred to let things stand as they were. In time, they began to write against each other, airing their incomprehensible feud in

F. Scott Fitzgerald, Zelda, and Scottie.

cially grateful for her interest in his own writing which differed so from hers. "The real people like Gertrude Stein," he said, "have a respect for people whose material may not touch theirs *at a single point*."

Anderson, Hemingway, and Fitzgerald were the key American literary figures in Gertrude Stein's life during the 1920s, but countless others came to pay homage at the rue de Fleurus as well. With some, such as the novelist and critic Robert Coates, she built lasting friendships; others, such as novelist Glenway Wescott, were abruptly dismissed—"He has a certain syrup, but it does not pour," she said of him.

Conspicuously absent from Gertrude Stein's circle were the three giant figures of the time—T. S. Eliot, Ezra Pound, and James Joyce. Yet, she met and had an opportunity to know all three. The meeting with Eliot was of no great interest to either. The hearty enthusiastic woman found she had little in common with the rather somber and sober poet. They discussed grammar, and when Eliot asked her on what authority she used split infinitives, Gertrude simply replied, "Henry James." Eliot frankly did not like her writing, though in his lectures to students he did acknowledge its significance.

Her lack of rapport with Ezra Pound is more puzzling. They were both literary pioneers, both passionately interested in young writers and most generous in giving them help and advice. After their first meeting, Gertrude said that she liked Pound but "did not find him amusing." The second meeting, however, was disastrous. Pound chose to talk of Japanese prints, Oriental music, and political economy, subjects that not only bored Gertrude but also irritated her, reminding her of some of Leo's interests. Pound's manner, too—his nervousness and compulsive talking—brought back unpleasant memories of Ger-

92   Ezra Pound in the garden of his Latin Quarter studio, Paris, 1923.

trude's brother. Thoroughly distasteful to Gertrude, as well, was Pound's presumptuous attempt to explain the paintings that hung on *her* wall. When, in a state of violent excitement, Pound fell out of her favorite armchair, she knew she would never invite him to her home again.

As for James Joyce, Gertrude's relationship, or lack of relationship, with him is a curious part of the history of twentieth century literature. Joyce was the star, the idol of the avant-garde, and he and Gertrude had many friends in common. They also lived near each other for many years. Yet they met only once, at the home of Jo Davidson, and their meeting was polite but without meaning. It is said that Gertrude felt they were moving in opposite directions artistically. While Joyce was utilizing the myths of the past in his writing, as well as creating new words and borrowing others from different languages, Gertrude was determined to break with the past, to use only her own language but in a new way. Thus, the gulf between them was enormous and permitted no contact between them. Her resentment of what the brilliant Irishman was writing is made clear by the fact that she gave up her subscription to Shakespeare and Company's lending library as soon as Sylvia Beach published Joyce's *Ulysses*.

Though Gertrude's most vital relationships during the 1920s were with other writers, she still continued her lively interest in painting. The influential role she had played in the careers of Matisse and Picasso was still remembered, and she remained, as the writer Ford Madox Ford said, "both Pope and Pharaoh of the picture-buying world." Her opinions were sought, and her appearance

Alice B. Toklas and Gertrude Stein in the studio at 27, rue de Fleurus, 1922.

at the exhibition of the work of a new painter was considered significant. However, it cannot be said that she made any particularly noteworthy discoveries during this period. She continued to number painters among her friends, and many of them followed Picasso's lead and used her as subject matter for their work—notably the sculptors Jacques Lipchitz and Jo Davidson. She showed interest in and bought works by the surrealists André Masson and Francis Picabia, and for a while expressed guarded enthusiasm for a group of neoromantics, led by the Russian-born Pavel Tchelitchew.

Her most rewarding new friendship with a painter during the 1920s was with the Spaniard Juan Gris. She had first met the young painter, who was to follow Picas-

Alice B. Toklas, Pavel Tchelitchew, and Gertrude Stein.

Juan Gris.

so's Cubism and then further develop it, in 1910 or 1911, but she didn't become interested in his work until a few years later. Then, she was one of the first to buy his paintings, a milestone in the life of the desperately poor young artist. Through a series of misunderstandings, the two quarreled in 1914, and it was not until 1921 that they reconciled and again became friends.

This time the friendship deepened, causing even Picasso to show signs of jealousy. Gris was a frequent visitor to the rue de Fleurus, and Gertrude admired, understood, and bought his work. She suggested to journalists that they write about him and did all she could to spread his fame. Gris grew to depend on her advice. "No one will write better about my painting than yourself," he told her in 1924. To show his gratitude, he executed designs for covers for chairs and stools in her home, which Alice then reproduced in needlework.

In 1926, Gris illustrated one of Gertrude's short works, "As a Wife Has a Cow," subsequently published in Paris, thereby formally linking their names together. When in 1927 Juan Gris died, at the age of forty, Gertrude was heartbroken. His life had been a tragic one of illness, poverty, and despair. His work had gone largely unappreciated, and at the time of his death his smaller paintings were selling for the equivalent of twenty dollars. Gertrude mourned deeply, and she wrote touchingly about her friend: "Therein Juan Gris is not everything but more than anything."

Chapter 8

GERTRUDE STEIN'S SOCIAL ROLE HAD CHANGED DURING THE 1920s, when she became a literary mother-nurse to a new generation; yet her own work concerned her most, then as always. Her working habits were not as rigid as they had been in the past though hardly a day passed without her doing at least some writing. She no longer worked all night; instead she generally arose no later than nine in the morning, bathed, dressed, read, wrote letters, and played with her dog until lunchtime. It was then time to go out—for a walk, for a drive in the car, or for some window-shopping. Wherever she went, she talked with the people around her and listened with her usual interest. No fixed appointments were ever arranged until after four in the afternoon.

Her writing could take place at any time and under any circumstances whether it was while posing for an artist doing her portrait, or in her new Ford, Godiva (so named because it was totally bare of extras), waiting while Alice took care of the shopping for the household.

Publication was still a problem for her enormous output, but during the 1920s her work was somewhat more available to the public than it had been, due largely to the growing importance of the "little magazines." These magazines, usually underfinanced and with circulations of rarely more than a few thousand, were the most vital factors in American literature. They were willing to publish new and experimental works by writers who were shunned by the larger commercial publications. Indeed, there were few, if any, American writers of significance who were not first published by these small but courageous periodicals.

Their names were indicative of their independent approaches to literature. In America, there was *Contact* and *Laughing Horse* and *S4N* and *Bozart*; as well as *Double-Dealer* and *Fugitive*, both of which brought the public the works of the increasingly important southern writers. And in Europe, the temporary American expatriates founded *Gargoyle* and *Secession* and *This Quarter*, and Ezra Pound organized *Exile*, which published some of his own best work along with that of Hemingway and the poet Louis Zukofsky.

Gertrude's writing, especially the shorter pieces she worked on during the 1920s, was particularly well suited to these small but influential magazines; through them her literature could become as well known as her reputation had. *The Oxford Magazine*, run by English college students, published a number of her articles; *The Reviewer*, an American publication, printed "Indian Boy"; and an annual American collection of poetry and fiction called *The American Caravan* published "Mildred's Thoughts." *The Little Review*, which had been among the early publishers of the works of Joyce, Eliot, Pound, and Hemingway and Anderson, agreed to print several of Gertrude's pieces, and *Broom* (so called because it meant to make a clean sweep of the past), a Rome-based magazine headed by the poet Alfred Kreymborg and Harold Loeb, included Gertrude's "If You Had Three Husbands" in one of its issues.

Of all the little magazines, three were most probably of the greatest value: *Criterion*, *Transatlantic Review*, and *transition*, and Gertrude's writing appeared in all three. *Criterion* was edited by T. S. Eliot, who somewhat begrudgingly and without too much enthusiasm agreed to publish a piece of Gertrude's—if it was her very latest. Gertrude, with some irony, immediately went to work on a portrait of Eliot and called it "November 15," the day he had asked for her most recent work. But *Criterion* didn't print it for nearly two years.

Transatlantic Review was edited by the distinguished English writer Ford Madox Ford, and Hemingway was one of his assistants. It had published Joyce and many of Ford's own works, and Hemingway convinced the editor to include excerpts from *The Making of Americans*, thereby giving the public the first chance to read at least some of what Gertrude considered her masterpiece.

Of most impact of all these magazines, however, was *transition*, a monthly edited by Elliot Paul and Eugene Jolas, the former a close friend of Gertrude's. Among the contributors were Joyce, Hemingway, e. e. cummings, and Hart Crane. Included, too, in its issues were some of Gertrude's best work—"The Life and Death of Juan Gris," "As a Wife Has a Cow A Love Story," and, in 1927, her first attempt to explain her style and literary approach, "An Elucidation."

These little magazines played a great part in building the reputation of Gertrude Stein. But theirs was a select and a limited readership, and what she wanted the most was to have her work published in book form, so that it might reach a larger public. Unfortunately, though her fame had spread, most publishers were still not interested in her work: it was not commercial. There were a few exceptions. In 1922, at the suggestion of Kate Buss, a journalist and admirer from Medford, Massachusetts, a collection of some of Gertrude's pieces, written between 1908 and 1920, was published by the Four Seas Company in Boston. Though Sherwood Anderson wrote a highly laudatory introduction, the volume, called *Geography and Plays,* had little success.

A few years later, Gertrude met a young American named Robert McAlmon. He was a poet and novelist himself, active in the publication of the avant-garde writers of the period. He had money, too, and in 1922 he had formed a publishing house in Paris called Contact Editions. *The Making of Americans* seemed ideal for the new house, and Gertrude convinced McAlmon that he should publish it. What should have been a high point in her career turned out to be a difficult and often painful experience. The enormous manuscript was sent to a French printer who specialized in setting type for foreign-language books—he had had the difficult job of printing Joyce's *Ulysses.* But when the proofs arrived, it was clear that the job had just been too difficult for the compositor. In addition to hundreds of normal errors in setting, he had taken it upon himself to correct what he thought were careless repetitions in the manuscript. Thus Alice and Gertrude were forced to spend an entire summer carefully checking the proofs word by word and making the corrections in such a way that the compositor might understand them. There was one consolation for Gertrude— in rereading *The Making of Americans,* she was more than ever convinced that she had written a masterpiece.

When the book was finally printed and published in

France, Gertrude was pleased and excited. But in her enthusiasm she argued with McAlmon, antagonizing him to such an extent that he would never again publish her work. She had admittedly gone too far in trying to promote and sell the book, and she agreed that McAlmon's anger was justified. She called herself "impulsive and slow-minded," and said, "Undoubtedly a great many complications have been the result."

In 1928, another solution to the problem of finding a permanent publisher seemed at hand. A representative for a seemingly courageous house in New York called Payson and Clarke expressed a desire to publish a collection of Gertrude's works, largely those dealing with American subjects or themes. She went through everything she had written from 1915 to 1926 and selected twenty-one pieces. Her hopes were high when the collection was published in New York under the title *Useful Knowledge*, but once again the book sold few copies and the publisher lacked the courage to go on publishing books by Gertrude Stein.

Book publishers did lack courage, Gertrude and Alice agreed. Why was it that art galleries would so often go to the expense and trouble of exhibiting paintings that would be inevitably difficult to sell while book publishers would not show enough faith in an author to publish his or her unconventional works? Something had to be done, and Alice decided to do it herself. She would learn all there was to know about publishing—it seemed merely a matter of printing a book and then selling it—and she would become a publisher. Gertrude enthusiastically agreed with this plan, so much so that she financed the new publishing house—Plain Editions—with the money she received from the sale of one of her favorite Picassos, *Girl with a Fan.*

Alice set out to learn all she could about her new profession. First of all, she was told she must subscribe to *Publishers' Weekly*, a magazine devoted to news of the publishing world that was essential reading for all American publishers. Then, she had to get a good list of booksellers to whom she could send circulars and order forms. Finally, armed with the knowledge she had picked up from *Publishers' Weekly* and supplied with a reasonably up-to-date list of American bookstores, she went to work. But it wasn't as easy as she expected. Printing and binding were expensive, advertising essential to the sale of the books was expensive, and all of this meant that the retail price of the books would be too high to appeal to the young people and artists who were the public for Gertrude's work. How, too, could she see to it that the books were reviewed in important newspapers and magazines? Problems multiplied daily but five of Gertrude Stein's books did appear under the imprint of Alice's Plain Editions. The first was a novel, *Lucy Church Amiably*, but unfortunately the book's appearance did not please its publisher. There were too many typographical errors, and it was poorly printed. The binding, too, was unsatisfactory: the book wouldn't stay closed, and its back broke.

Lucy Church Amiably was a typical example of one direction that Gertrude's writing was taking during the

1920s. While an increasing number of her articles tried to explain to the reader her attempts to solve her own problems of language and style, her other writings were concerned with details of country life, of the joys and romance of nature. *Lucy Church Amiably* is a perfect example of the latter, and the "Advertisement" in the front of the book sets its mood and tone:

Lucy Church Amiably. There is a church and it is in Lucey and it has a steeple and the steeple is a pagoda and there is no reason for it and it looks like something else. Besides this there is amiably and this comes from the paragraph.

Select your song she said and it was done and then she said and it was done with a nod and then she bent her head in the direction of the falling water. Amiably.

This altogether makes a return to romantic nature that is it makes a landscape look like an engraving in which there were some people, after all if they are to be seen there they feel as pretty as they look and this makes it have a river a gorge an inundation and a remarkable meadowed mass which is whatever they use not to feed but to bed cows. Lucy Church Amiably is a novel of romantic beauty and nature and of Lucy Church and John Mary and Simon Therese.

The simple pleasures of nature and country living had always appealed to Gertrude; even as a young girl she had enjoyed leaving the city to walk through the calm and peaceful countryside. As she grew older, an escape from the city became increasingly necessary. Playing her role as a kind of literary oracle in Paris was exhausting and more and more she looked forward each year to the summer when she could leave her Parisian activities behind.

In 1922, she and Alice went to Saint-Rémy, a charming town in Provence. It was quiet and restful, and when not writing Gertrude spent her time visiting neighboring villages and chatting with the hardworking farmers. Her writing during this period was lyrical, and her subjects often bees and sheep and donkeys and water and trees. There too she wrote "An Elucidation," the examination of her own methods of creation which was later published in *transition*. She enjoyed her time at Saint-Rémy so much that the two women remained far past the summer —until March, when the bad weather came to Provence.

The following summer was to be spent near Picasso, at Antibes, on the French Riviera. The two were once again very close. "She and Picasso were phenomenal together," wrote Gerald Murphy, a close friend of Scott Fitzgerald's. "Each stimulated the other to such an extent that everyone felt recharged witnessing it." Gertrude then had an opportunity to meet the painter's mother, and she told her that her son had been "remarkably beautiful" when she first met him—"illuminated as if he wore a halo." Picasso's mother replied that he had been even more beautiful as a young boy. "And now?" asked the painter. Now, Gertrude and his mother jokingly agreed, "there is no such beauty left."

Life by the sea and the movement of the waves delighted Gertrude just as life in the farm country had, but the following summer she and Alice decided to return to stay at a small town they had passed through on their way to the Riviera. Belley, with its five thousand inhabitants, had charmed them at once. The landscape and the people and the trees and the oxen made it a perfect place in which to go about the wearying task of correcting the proofs of *The Making of Americans* which had to be read the summer of 1924. It more than fulfilled all their expectations, and they returned there enthusiastically each summer. By 1926, they decided to find a house in the area, one in which they might live half of each year. This house was spotted by Gertrude as she looked across the valley from the terrace of the hotel in which they were staying. Though she saw it only from the distance, her mind was made up, and she investigated the possibilities of moving into it as soon as possible. She learned to her disappointment that the house was occupied by a French army officer; but the real estate agent, a kindly old farmer, promised her that as soon as the house was vacated— inevitably the officer would be transferred to another post— the house would be hers.

By 1929, it was, and when she and Alice saw it they realized that they had been right in their choice. Situated in the tiny village of Bilignin, nothing more than a cluster of houses and farmhouses on a winding country road, it was a beautiful old manor house, with a large courtyard and an immense garden in which Alice could work raising all of her favorite vegetables. On the terrace, with its imposing view of the valley, Gertrude could stretch out on a deck chair, resting and thinking and pondering on her career as a writer.

During these years, she thought more and more of the difficulties that readers were having in understanding her work, and tried in many ways to explain her own creative process and aims. An unusual opportunity to do this to a young and receptive audience presented itself in the fall of 1925, when the president of the Cambridge Literary Society wrote asking her to speak before the society in the spring of 1926. Public appearances frightened her, so much so that she had no difficulty in turning down the invitation.

However, her close friend Edith Sitwell intervened. Miss Sitwell was a well-known English poet, famous for her wit and irony, as well as for her enormous height and distinguished nose. She and her brothers Osbert and Sacheverell, also writers, children of a noble Norman and English family, were forceful and influential figures in British intellectual life. She had in 1923 written what Gertrude thought to be a very condescending review of *Geography and Plays*, but a year later she had reconsidered and published an article highly praising Gertrude's writing. When Edith Sitwell came to Paris, she and Gertrude immediately became good and understanding friends.

Edith Sitwell was shocked to learn that Gertrude had turned down the invitation from Cambridge. What better chance would she have to reach an intelligent public and thereby spread her fame? In addition, she had arranged for Gertrude to speak at Oxford a few days after the Cambridge lecture. She wrote all this so forcefully to her friend in Paris that Gertrude changed her mind and

Edith Sitwell.

agreed to speak at England's two most distinguished universities. However, it was one thing to agree and another actually to do it. She didn't know what to say, and even if she did, she was afraid to get up and say it to a large and curious audience. Her first problem was soon solved. After many, many days of considering her subject matter for the lectures, she was suddenly inspired—in a garage, while waiting for one of Godiva's many repair jobs to be completed. There she wrote the text of her lecture, and she called it "Composition as Explanation."

Once she had completed it, there remained the problem of how to deliver it. All her friends had to listen to her read it, and all were asked advice; and none agreed. By one friend she was told to speak as slowly as possible and never look down; another advised her to talk as quickly as possible and never look up.

In the spring of 1926, Gertrude and Alice went to England. Upon their arrival, the Sitwells had a party in Gertrude's honor. However, Gertrude's mind was not on parties; she was nervously preoccupied with the tortures she would undergo while delivering her speech in Cambridge the following day. Osbert Sitwell did his best to comfort her, explaining the various symptoms of stage fright and the possible ways of combatting it.

The next day, after tea and dinner with the president of the Cambridge Literary Society and selected guests, Gertrude was led to the lecture room. Dressed in a blue Chinese brocaded robe that Alice had ordered for the occasion, she nervously mounted the platform. But as she began to speak, her nervousness disappeared. Soon, she was completely at ease. The students listened carefully and attentively, and when she finished they applauded enthusiastically. Even more satisfying was the question period that followed during which Gertrude handled herself with her usual assurance and charm.

By the time she was scheduled to speak at Oxford, there was no longer a question of being nervous. It was a beautiful spring day, and an enormous audience, with numerous standees, greeted her appearance. She was, according to one member of the audience, "a squat Aztec figure in obsidian, growing more monumental as she sat down."

This "Aztec figure in obsidian" cast an immediate spell over the students; she charmed them even more than she had charmed those at Cambridge. However, during the animated one-hour discussion period that followed the lecture, it was clear that some young men had come to heckle her, to make fun of her. To them she was a joke and her writing was not to be taken seriously. Nonetheless, there was not a single question that Gertrude could not answer intelligently, and at each point she demonstrated her wit and sensitive powers of perception. If not all of the students present left the hall convinced of her importance as a writer, and if many of them could still not understand what she wrote, they were certain of her seriousness as an artist and of her sincerity in attempting to create a new literature.

Indeed, during the 1920s, more and more people were convinced of Gertrude Stein's sincerity of purpose. By 1926, Janet Flanner, under the name Genêt, wrote in *The New Yorker:* "No American writer is taken more seriously than Miss Stein by Paris modernists." In 1931, America's most influential literary critic, Edmund Wilson, wrote a book called *Axel's Castle*, an appraisal and study of those writers he considered to be of the greatest significance of the period. Along with essays on Eliot, Yeats, Valéry, Proust, and Joyce, he included one on Gertrude Stein. The French, too, were beginning to appreciate her, and translations were published of some of the portraits as well as excerpts from *The Making of Americans*, and a selection of "Melanchtha." A leading French critic, Marcel Brion, wrote an article stating that she was to literature what Bach was to music. Another, Bernard Faÿ, who was to become her great friend, wrote: "Her books are filled with ideas, but in place of freeing her ideas and expressing them as ideas, which would have been the method of a French writer, Miss Stein keeps all her ideas alive and mixed with the facts that bear them, and also she keeps all her facts richly filled with ideas. She has lived, felt and understood so intensely and so clearly all the fact of her life that in truth her life is no more simply visited with a few ideas but is a living continuous essential idea."

Yet the publishers and the public lagged behind. In the years following World War I, an outstanding number of books were written that are now considered modern classics: *Ulysses, The Waste Land, The Enormous Room,* and *The Garden Party* were all published in one year—1922. And throughout the decade, Hemingway wrote *The Sun Also Rises* and *A Farewell to Arms;* Fitzgerald wrote *The Beautiful and Damned* and *The Great Gatsby;* Faulkner wrote *The Sound and the Fury,* and John Dos Passos *Three Soldiers.*

These distinguished writers had all reached the public

they deserved. They were read as well as spoken of. Only Gertrude Stein was missing from the list. It is true that she was certainly spoken of, though often in jest, but she was not read. Her fame was largely that of a personality, and it was not of that that she had dreamed.

Somehow, in some way, she would have to write a book that could reach the public and bring her immortality.

Chapter 9

By the summer of 1932, Gertrude had her beloved house in Bilignin and had a devoted white poodle with blue eyes and a pink nose which she had found at a neighborhood dog show and promptly named Basket. She also had a marvelous new car—the aging Godiva, she had written to a friend, "took to dropping little pieces of herself and groaning distressfully and once had to be disgracefully rocked in front of the Senate and now I am having a new Ford car and with all the unfaithfulness characteristic of us all I am violently . . . devoted to the new."

Thus, the atmosphere was right for Gertrude to write the book that was to bring her the fame she had so long desired. It had started almost as a joke, with Gertrude urging Alice to write her autobiography and Alice saying no, and then Gertrude decided that she, Gertrude Stein, would write *The Autobiography of Alice B. Toklas*. She would tell the story as simply as Defoe had told the story of Robinson Crusoe, but it would be her own story, inevitably linked with Alice's, told in what would have been Alice's words, reflecting Alice's point of view and attitude and language.

The result is a completely delightful book, a perceptive and amusing portrait of Gertrude Stein, of her friends, and of the period in which she lived. There was no question of obscure meanings or difficulties in the text: it was a book that any literate person could read with pleasure, proof—if proof was needed—that Gertrude Stein could write simply and clearly, if the occasion called for it.

The response to it was immediate, and enthusiastic. One of Gertrude's dreams had been publication in the

Alice and Gertrude in open car.

Atlantic Monthly magazine. For years the editors of the *Atlantic* had rejected her work, but not this time. "There has been a lot of pother about this book of yours," the editor wrote her, "but what a delightful book it is, and how glad I am to publish four installments of it! During our correspondence, I think you felt my constant hope that the time would come when the real Miss Stein would pierce the smokescreen with which she has always so mischievously surrounded herself. The autobiography has just enough of the oblique to give it individuality and character, and readers who care for the things you do will love it. . . .

"Hail Gertrude Stein about to arrive!"

Gertrude was overjoyed but also slightly puzzled. Hadn't she always been the "real Gertrude Stein"? For the moment, it didn't matter. As soon as serialization of the book began, fan letters arrived daily from America. Money started to come in, too, more than she had ever had. She bought herself another Ford and an expensive new coat and two studded collars for Basket. When the book itself was published, there was more praise, extravagant praise from all the critics as well as the public, which made *The Autobiography of Alice B. Toklas* an enormous best seller. There were some negative reactions, too, especially from Leo whose important role in Gertrude's life was ignored in the autobiography. "What a liar she is!" he wrote to Mabel Weeks, complaining of the factual errors he found in the book. To another friend, Ettie Stettheimer, he wrote: "Nothing of the pre-war period is accurately true, very little of the whole is accurately true, and very little of it is approximately true." But Gertrude readily admitted that her memory was not perfect, and in any case she was enjoying her success too much to let Leo's comments bother her.

However, her state of euphoria could not last forever. The question of who the real Gertrude Stein was worried her. "Everything in living is made up of finding out what you are," she said, and this was now questioned. "All of a sudden I was not just I because so many people did know me . . . I was no longer I." Having the money was marvelous, and she admitted "I do want to get rich but I never want to do what there is to do to get rich."

Worst of all, she couldn't seem to write: she was blocked, and nothing came out the way she wanted it to. She had often accused other writers of becoming sterile when they reached success, but now she understood. "I had blamed them. . . . Now I know better. It does cut off your flow." Writing had been at the center of her life, and without it she was off balance. Everything seemed to annoy her, as she uncharacteristically became involved in household details at Bilignin. Guests bothered her—they stayed too long. Village happenings, which had formerly amused her, began to irritate her. She started to work on a new book, a kind of detective story, while in the country and continued working on it in Paris, but it was unsatisfactory. "Although I did it, I did not really do it," she commented. Too much of her time was spent in being a celebrity, and what hurt her writing the most was a newfound feeling that she must write for the public, and not necessarily what she wanted to write. "I began to think," she wrote, "about how my writing would sound to others, how I could make them understand, I who always lived within myself and my writing." This new attitude was dangerous and could destroy her as a writer.

Yet there were the inevitable compensations, in addition to the money and fame she enjoyed. Now American publishers were eager to publish her work, and when her agent, William Bradley, went to New York she instructed him to sell all he could, but to sell *The Making of Americans* first—which he soon did, in a shortened version. The success of *The Autobiography of Alice B. Toklas* also led to the production of her first opera, and one of the works for which she is best known today. It is titled *Four Saints in Three Acts*, and is the result of a collaboration with the American composer Virgil Thomson.

Gertrude had first met Thomson during the winter of 1925–1926. He had read all of her published writing and was deeply impressed. Gertrude too was impressed with his talent as well as his perceptive understanding of her writing, and a warm friendship developed. Thomson had set some of Gertrude's poetry to music, and she was delighted with the results, so much so that she responded favorably when the composer suggested they work together on an opera. First, however, they had to agree on a subject and after considering and rejecting themes in American history, they came upon the idea of saints. It would be saints, and the setting would be Spain, and in this way Gertrude could bring to the work her knowledge of and devotion to Saint Teresa. By July 1927, Gertrude had finished the libretto, and in 1928 Virgil Thomson

Virgil Thomson.

finished the score. But in spite of all their efforts, it seemed impossible to raise enough interest and money in the project to enable the production to come to life.

By 1933, Gertrude Stein was a best-selling author; anything of hers was of interest, so the money was raised for a production of the opera. Since Gertrude was in Paris and Thomson in America, Thomson was responsible for seeing to all the many details involved in bringing a complex and unconventional work to the stage. There was friction between the collaborators—largely arguments over contractual details, since Gertrude's famous sense of humor did not apply to financial matters—but the production plans went ahead. The opening was to take place in the auditorium of the Avery Memorial, a new wing of the Wadsworth Atheneum, a major museum in Hartford, Connecticut, on February 8, 1934. In conjunction with the opera's opening, there was to be a major retrospective showing of Picasso's work, the first to be held in America.

It was in every way a major cultural event. On February 7 and 8, the New Haven Railroad put on extra cars from New York to accommodate the notables that would go to Hartford for the opening. The theatre was packed, and the audience awaited with an air of excitement before the curtain rose. What they saw and heard was far from an ordinary opera, but a wholly captivating work of striking originality. Visually, the production was splendid. There were trees made out of feathers and a sea wall made out of shells. The stage was bathed in bright white light, illuminating the cellophane and white gauze backgrounds. The cast, made up of black actors and singers, sang beautifully and moved gracefully, before a sky-blue background and among pink palm trees.

When read, the Stein text is as difficult to follow as her most difficult work, but somehow the words when sung conveyed an undeniable feeling of gaiety and charm. The theme of the opera is the religious life. The action, set in sixteenth century Spain, consists of incidents in the lives of Saint Teresa and Saint Ignatius. Instead of four saints, there are more than thirty, and instead of three acts, there are four—but that was to be expected in an opera that contained a famous Stein phrase, "Pigeons on the grass alas," and began with the words:

> *To know to know to love her so.*
> *Four saints prepare for saints.*
> *It makes it well fish.*
> *Four saints it makes it well fish.*

The audience responded warmly to Gertrude's singable libretto and to Thomson's lyrical score, which set everything of Gertrude's to music, even her stage directions. There were six performances in Hartford, after which the production was moved to New York. More singers were added to the cast, a few more instruments added to the orchestra, and minor revisions in the staging made before all was ready for the Broadway production.

The opening in New York fell on one of the coldest nights of the year; the streets were icy, and to make things even more difficult, there was a taxi strike. Nonetheless, everyone of importance in the New York theatrical and musical world, from George Gershwin to Arturo Toscanini, managed to attend.

The audience, whether they understood the opera or not, clearly had a good time. The reviews were mixed, with the usual number of critics making fun of Gertrude's eccentric libretto. But it was a hit; for more than six months, *Four Saints in Three Acts* was mentioned at least once a week in every New York newspaper. There were editorials, cartoons, and jokes: but after *The Autobiography of Alice B. Toklas* and *Four Saints in Three Acts*, there was no doubt that Gertrude Stein was a major celebrity.

To the question of when she would return to America, Gertrude had always replied: "Not until I am a lion." She was now a lion and was besieged with lucrative offers to return to the States to lecture. She found it difficult to make up her mind. Having been away a long time, she felt in some ways out of touch with the America she had left almost thirty years before. A return would be a search for roots, and she wasn't sure that she wanted to undertake that search. Then, too, there was the fear that the American public would look upon her as a curiosity, caring more about her eccentricities than about her writing. She was unable to understand this. "After all," she wrote, "there is no sense in it because if it were not for my work they would not be interested in me so why should they not be more interested in my work than in me."

On the other hand, she had good friends in America and looked forward to seeing them. The always faithful Carl Van Vechten urged her to make the trip. Scott Fitzgerald, too, thought the trip a good idea and wrote her that if she came to Baltimore "You have one devoted

slave in this vicinity who tenders you material homage."
In addition, Sherwood Anderson thought she should have
"one big tasty square meal of America again."

In spite of Gertrude's misgivings and fears, she and
Alice set out for America in October 1934. She had prepared six lectures to be given throughout the country and
was confident that she had made a wise decision. This
was her chance not only to see her country again, but
perhaps to show the American people that she must be
taken seriously as a writer.

Upon her arrival on the *S. S. Champlain*, she was
greeted by a mob of reporters, an encounter which set
the tone for her relationship with the press for the rest
of her visit. They came expecting a kind of madwoman,
and they were sure they could turn out amusing stories
making fun of her. Instead, they found an earthy, warm,
and intelligent woman. "Why don't you write the way
you talk?" one asked. "Why don't you read the way I
write?" she responded. And she went on: "I do talk as I
write, but you can hear better than you can see. You are
accustomed to see with your eyes differently to the way
you hear with your ears, and perhaps that is what makes
it hard to read my works."

Every question she was asked was answered with wit
and intelligence. She charmed the most cynical reporter,
and in turn the press turned out endless copy on her every
comment and move during her stay in America. The day
she arrived the moving lights that gave the news of the
world from the New York Times Building flashed the
word that Gertrude Stein had arrived. People, drawn by

her admittedly strange costumes as well as by the enormous publicity that was accorded her in the press, stopped her in the streets to talk. Everything she said was quoted, repeated, and commented upon. She was indeed a lion.

From New York, Alice and Gertrude, accompanied by Carl Van Vechten, took their first plane trip—to Chicago. There they would see the production of *Four Saints* and Gertrude would lecture at the university. The plane ride made a profound impression, and she later wrote: "When I was in America I for the first time traveled pretty much all the time in an airplane and when I looked at the earth I saw all the lines of cubism made at a time when not any painter had ever gone up in an airplane. I saw there on the earth the mingling lines of Picasso, coming and going, developing and destroying themselves, I saw the simple solutions of Braque, I saw the wandering lines of Masson, yes I saw and once more I knew that a creator is contemporary, he understands what is contemporary when the contemporaries do not yet know it, but he is contemporary and as the twentieth century is a century which sees the earth as no one has ever seen it, the earth has a splendor that it never has had, and as everything destroys itself in the twentieth century and nothing continues, so then the twentieth century has a splendor which is its own and Picasso is of this century, he has that strange quality of an earth that one has never seen and of things destroyed as they have never been destroyed. So then Picasso has his splendor."

Shortly after arriving in Chicago, Gertrude, Alice and Van Vechten went to the gigantic Auditorium Theatre to

Gertrude and Alice departing for Chicago to see *Four Saints in Three Acts*. The fetishes they are holding, given to them by Carl Van Vechten, are little beaded men of rabbits' feet, made by the Hopi Indians.

see the already celebrated production of *Four Saints*. Gertrude was the reigning star of the evening and was placed in the center box of honor. She thoroughly enjoyed her position, but her hearing had been temporarily impaired by her first plane ride and she couldn't hear the words she had written from the box, so she was moved to an orchestra seat. She was pleased with what she saw and heard and delighted with the attention paid her by the press after the performance.

Her lecture at the University of Chicago, too, was a complete success. It had been arranged for by her devoted friend Thornton Wilder, who was teaching at the university at the time. The administration was so pleased with her lecture and student reaction to it that she was invited to conduct ten seminar sessions. It seemed a perfect chance to explain her work to an eager group of students, and she took advantage of it.

She had created a style, a manner of writing that came to be known as "Steinese," after its creator. To her it was simple and legitimate. Words were used not only for their literal meanings but for their sounds and associations. Conventional punctuation and syntax seemed to her an obstacle toward the expression of what she wanted to convey. Her much laughed-at repetition was in fact a series of variations which helped her present her impressions and a state of mind. Her method was a serious one, carefully thought out, yet she was too often made fun of. Thus, when at the University of Chicago, she was asked for the meaning of her famous "a rose is a rose is a rose is a rose," she was glad to have the chance to explain clear-

Gertrude Stein and Thornton Wilder at Bilignin.

ly, so that even those who had scoffed—"A pose is a pose is a pose"—could understand.

"Now listen. Can't you see that when the language was new—as it was with Chaucer and Homer—the poet could use the name of a thing and the thing was really there. And can't you see that after hundreds of years had gone by and thousands of poems had been written, he could call on those words and find that they were just wornout literary words. The excitingness of pure being had been

Gertrude at the home of Mrs. Charles Goodspeed during her visit to Chicago.

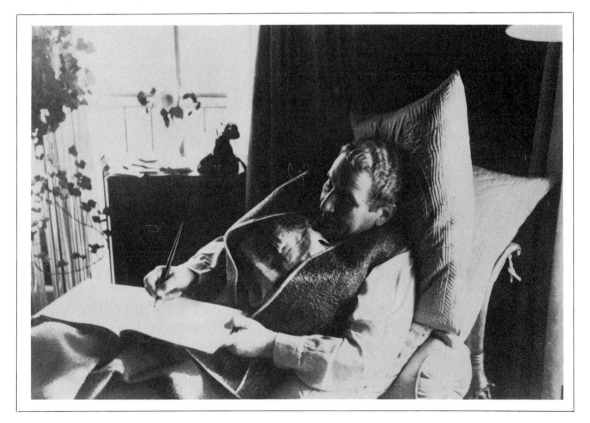

withdrawn from them; they were just rather stale literary words. Now the poet has to work in the excitingness of pure being; he has to get back that intensity into the language. We all know that it's hard to write poetry in a late age; and we know that you have to put some strangeness, as something unexpected, into the structure of the sentence in order to bring back vitality to the noun. Now it's not enough to be bizarre; the strangeness in the sentence has to come from the poetic gift, too. That's why it's doubly hard to be a poet in a late age. Now you all have seen hundreds of poems about roses and you know in your bones that the rose is not there. All those songs that sopranos sing as encores about 'I have a garden! oh, what a garden!' Now I don't want to put too much emphasis on that line, because it's just one line in a longer poem. But I notice that you all know it; you make fun of it, but you know it. Now listen! I'm no fool. I know that in daily life we don't go around saying '. . . is a . . . is a . . . is a . . .' Yes, I'm no fool; but I think that in that line the rose is red for the first time in English poetry for a hundred years."

From Chicago, Gertrude went to New England, then to the South, the Southwest, and on to California. She enjoyed seeing old friends like Scott Fitzgerald and Sherwood Anderson, but she didn't like to see the places of her past—they reminded her too much of the passage of time. Wherever she went, she was treated as a major celebrity: she had tea at the White House with Eleanor Roosevelt; George Gershwin played the score of *Porgy and Bess* for her on the piano; she met Charlie Chaplin and Mary Pickford in Hollywood; she cheered at a Yale-

Dartmouth football game; and was overwhelmed by the vastness of Yosemite. But after a few months, she had had enough. The endless lecturing and the almost daily interviews had begun to wear her out. It was time to go home.

As she was about to return to France, she asked Bennett Cerf, the brilliant and imaginative publisher of Random House, what he felt her publishing future should be. Cerf replied that she need merely choose one book a year, and he would publish whatever it was. The American trip had been a success: not only had she impressed and charmed all those with whom she came into contact, but she also had found a publisher who soundly believed in what she was doing.

Chapter 10

THE EUROPE TO WHICH GERTRUDE RETURNED WAS ONCE AGAIN preoccupied with thoughts of war, but for her all such talk was absurd. She already had been through one major war, and that was enough. What she wanted now was a chance to enjoy her newly found celebrity. Even the fact that twenty-five hundred French soldiers were stationed at tiny Bilignin—twenty-five of them billeted at her house —did not convince her that Europe was again preparing for battle.

The important thing was her fame which, even if she was puzzled by its meaning, she thoroughly enjoyed. More people than ever came to meet her and pay their respects, both in Paris and in Bilignin. The lost generation for the most part had found itself back in America so that much of the stimulation and excitement was gone, but Gertrude reveled in being a star attraction.

She wrote steadily, no longer having to worry about finding a publisher, and her style became somewhat easier to follow. Though still worried that she might actually lose her true identity by trying, even subconsciously, to reach the same wide public that had read *The Autobiography of Alice B. Toklas*, she did create works that were infinitely more accessible to the average reader than those she had written in the past. There was a charming short work called *Paris France*, largely concerned with the character of the French and the values of French civilization, and her first children's book, *The World Is Round*. Some of her writing was concerned with the problem of the search for identity, notably a work of nonfiction called *The Geographical History of America* and *Ida*, a novel

Gertrude at Bilignin with Pepe and Basket I.

whose heroine loses her true identity and becomes no more than a creation of publicity. She continued her own autobiography, too, calling this second volume *Everybody's Autobiography*—Alice B. Toklas had done hers, she reasoned, and now "anybody" will do "theirs."

Actually, none of these books reached that broad public

131

she wanted, in spite of her enormous fame. She had conquered America; she was practically an American monument in France; and in England where she returned to lecture at Oxford and Cambridge and where a ballet based on one of her plays was produced by the Sadler's Wells Company, she was one of the best known American writers.

Slowly, however, a rich period in her life was coming to an end. The apartment at 27, rue de Fleurus, which she had made world famous, was taken away from her, her landlord terminating her lease in order to give it to his son. "I guess 27 got so historical," she wrote to Sherwood Anderson, "it just could not hold us any longer," and she and Alice moved to a smaller apartment formerly occupied by Queen Christina of Sweden, at 5, rue Christine. The move meant examining much of her past, including her still-fabulous collection of paintings. Over the years when in need of money she had sold many of her valuable paintings but Janet Flanner, whom she asked to make an inventory at the time of the move, found there were still 138 canvases, of which 99 were hung on the walls.

At this time too, her devoted dog Basket died, at the age of ten. He had been her steady companion, she had written of him in her books and he had been a favorite of the children of the village of Bilignin, who called him Monsieur Basket. On his death, "we did cry and cry and everyone said get another dog and get it right away." Though Picasso said she must find a completely different kind of dog who in no way resembled Basket, Gertrude

Gertrude at 5, rue Christine.

Gertrude and Basket II.

chose another white poodle, whom she called Basket II. The villagers compared him to the first Basket but they never called him Monsieur.

Far more serious changes were to take place in Gertrude's life, but she seemed to close her eyes to all that was happening around her. In 1939, when the whole world was sure that war was about to begin, she wrote to an American magazine: "It does not seem possible for any of you to realize that most probably there will not be another general European war." Her friends urged her to send her paintings to America so that they might be safe, but she scoffed at their suggestions. Significantly, however, she did send her unpublished manuscripts to Carl Van Vechten for safekeeping in New York.

Gertrude and Alice were in Bilignin when on September 1 Hitler's troops invaded Poland. Two days later, France declared war on Germany, and a general conflict spread throughout the continent. It was no longer a question of what Gertrude wanted to believe, and the two women obtained a pass to return briefly to Paris to gather up their possessions before settling in the country for the duration of the war. Of her entire collection of paintings, Gertrude took only two with her: the Picasso portrait and Cézanne's portrait of Madame Cézanne. The rest remained in her apartment.

There had been no question of remaining in the capital. Life in the country would be far easier during the wartime and far less dangerous. Since she was able to block out anything that didn't concern her, it was a paradoxically peaceful period for Gertrude. She read detective stories which she had always enjoyed, and she took long walks, this time with Basket II. The villagers became her friends, and she liked sharing their simple lives. Alice took care of and expanded the garden, thereby assuring a supply of food. She gathered fruit, made jam, and concocted new, improvised dishes for Gertrude's pleasure. To give Gertrude the meals she wanted, Alice had learned to kill carp and smother pigeons (the French are opposed to neck-wringing, since the loss of blood, they feel, causes a loss of flavor).

At night, the village was blacked out as the threat of German bombs was a serious one, but Gertrude was comforted by a neighbor who told her that Bilignin, being in the foothills of the Alps, would be difficult to find from the air. Nonetheless, bombs had fallen nearby, and Gertrude did her best to keep her mind off them by writing children's books and following the optimistic predictions of an astrologer named Leonardo Blake.

The optimism was unfounded, however, as the German army overran Europe. Paris itself was occupied by the invaders in June 1940, and the position of Gertrude and Alice was a dangerous one. They were two elderly Jewish, American women, who could very well have been taken off to a Nazi concentration camp. At one point, they telephoned the American Consul in Lyon who advised them to go to the consulate at once so that he might arrange for their immediate departure from France. At the last moment, they changed their minds, determined to "cut box hedges" in Bilignin and ignore the war that was surrounding them. A second time, Alice panicked, and the two women decided to face the inevitable and leave for Spain, but before they had a chance to leave a neighbor convinced them that they were better off in danger among friends than in safety among strangers.

On June 25, France's General Pétain signed an armistice with the Germans, turning the country over to a Fascist-oriented government. Still, Gertrude made no attempt to leave, not even when German soldiers occupied Belley. She was at first shocked to see them in her town, but she found them quiet and polite and they were good to Basket II. At three different times, German soldiers were quartered in her home, and it is easy to imagine what would have happened if they had discovered she was not only an American but a Jew. However, her French neighbors did their best to protect her; and her servants spoke to the invaders as much as possible so they would not be able to discover her American accent.

When the Germans finally left and French soldiers returned to the village, all seemed well again. Gertrude Stein was politically blind, and the fact that the world around her was in danger of crumbling did not seem to disturb her. She had friends in the collaborationist Vichy government which ruled the country, and they would take care of her. She had bread and butter and wine and vegetables and, occasionally, meat or fish, and she confidently believed that all would return to normal. Only toward the end of the war, when she came to know personally and to admire the courage of the maquis, the valiant French underground movement which was battling the Fascist government, did she realize her errors.

One June 6, 1944, Allied forces landed in Normandy in northern France; on August 15, additional Allied troops landed in the south. The liberation of France was at hand,

and the townspeople of Belley were enthusiastic at the impending arrival of American and British forces. No one was happier than Gertrude Stein when, on August 31, the first American soldiers arrived in Belley. There were three of them, whom she greeted with open arms. When she explained who she was, they offered her a ride in a jeep which she accepted joyfully.

Thus began her love affair with the American army. Each and every soldier was welcome in her home, and to each of them she gave warmth and sympathetic understanding. Once again, her maternal magnetism brought cheer to a generation of lost Americans. She had kept a journal of her life during the Occupation and had said she would end it the day the Americans arrived. So she did, eagerly sending it on to New York where it was published as *Wars I Have Seen.*

By the end of November, preparations were made for the return to Paris. She cabled Carl Van Vechten: "Joyous days endless love." In this mood she returned to the rue Christine, delighted to find that though vandals had been through the apartment, the precious paintings she had left on the walls had not been stolen. The day after her arrival, Picasso came and the two shared a tender and ecstatic reunion.

As she walked through the streets of Paris with Basket II all seemed the same as it had been. She suspected that the war years had been nothing but a long nightmare from which she had awakened without any bad effects.

As soon as her home was again livable, she opened its doors wide once again, this time to the American sol-

Gertrude and Alice with GI's at enlisted men's club.

diers who were stationed in or passed through Paris. She
stopped them on the street, she questioned them about
their homes and families and did her best to give them
a temporary home in a foreign city. "How we love the
American army we never do stop loving the American
army one single minute," she wrote. She went to army

mess halls to eat, she talked to attentive informal gatherings, exchanging ideas with men from all walks of life. She enjoyed their language and its flexibility and recorded it faithfully in a book she called *Brewsie and Willie*, a series of conversations among American soldiers.

When the army asked her to tour Belgium and American bases in occupied Germany, she accepted eagerly. In her talks, she was frank and strong-minded, angering many soldiers by her rigid, inflexible opinions, but forcing them to think—and in the end many agreed with her. Agree or not, they took comfort in her honesty and smile and laughter. After one lecture, she wrote to Van Vechten: "Enclosed is a description of a talk I gave them which did excite them, they walked me home fifty strong after the lecture was over and in the narrow streets of the quarter they made all the automobiles take side streets, the police looked and followed a bit but gave up."

It was an enriching experience for Gertrude as well as for the soldiers, but after a while she became inexplicably tired. Soldiers who had been welcomed so warmly at her apartment were turned away; all invitations were rejected. Gertrude had never been really sick and she refused to listen to the worried Alice who suggested illness might be the cause of her sudden fatigue. All she needed, she said, was a rest, and on July 19, 1946, the two women left Paris to stay at the home of a friend in the country. In the midst of the drive, Gertrude fainted, and she was rushed back to the American Hospital in Paris.

It was too late. She was dying of cancer, a cancer which

had been taking its toll for many years, perhaps even having started during her trip to America. On July 22, Alice presented her with the first copy of *Brewsie and Willie*. On the twenty-seventh, she was to undergo a hopeless operation. When she came out of the anaesthetic, she turned to the always faithful Alice B. Toklas and said, "What is the answer?" The heartbroken Alice was unable to reply and, after a pause, Gertrude went on: "In that case, what is the question?" These, it is said, were her last words.

As part of her will, Gertrude Stein bequeathed the portrait Picasso had given her in 1906 to New York's Metropolitan Museum of Art. Shortly before the painting was leaving the rue Christine for New York, Alice invited a very few friends in to see it. Among them was Picasso. Alice was there alone to greet him. He looked at the other paintings of his which lined the walls of the apartment but apparently paid little attention to Gertrude's portrait. But just before leaving, he went toward it, stood before it, and silently said farewell to his friend. He then kissed Alice—something he had rarely if ever done—and left.

Throughout her mature years, Gertrude Stein feared being remembered more as a personality than as a writer. With the exception of *The Autobiography of Alice B. Toklas*, and an occasional phrase like "A rose is a rose is a rose," this had been the case. Yet today, in 1973, more books by this extraordinary woman are available to the reading public than ever before—and in paperback editions, at low cost, and thus accessible to the young people she had hoped to reach. Is it possible that Sherwood

Anderson's words, written in 1922, were actually prophetic? "Would it not be a lovely and charmingly ironic gesture of the gods if, in the end, the work of this artist were to prove the most lasting and important of all the word slingers of our generation!"

Books by Gertrude Stein
For Further Reading
Photocredits
Index

Books by Gertrude Stein:

There are two excellent anthologies, both of them covering the complete range of Gertrude Stein's writing, and both available in paperback.

Selected Writings of Gertrude Stein, edited by Carl Van Vechten (New York, Vintage Books, 1972), includes, among other works, *The Autobiography of Alice B. Toklas, Tender Buttons*, "Composition as Explanation," "Melanctha," "Portrait of Mabel Dodge at the Villa Curonia," "Miss Furr and Miss Skeene," *Four Saints in Three Acts*, and excerpts from *The Making of Americans* and *Wars I Have Seen*, as well as some portraits and plays.

Gertrude Stein: Writings and Lectures, 1909–1945, edited by Patricia Meyerowitz (Baltimore, Penguin Books, 1971), includes, among other works, some of Gertrude Stein's most important lectures, *Tender Buttons*, ten of the Portraits, two of the plays, *Ida*, and excerpts from *Brewsie and Willie*.

Among the individual works at present available in paperback are the following:

The Autobiography of Alice B. Toklas (Vintage) (Random)
Geography & Plays (Something Else Press)
Ida (Vintage)
Lucy Church Amiably (Something Else Press)
The Making of Americans (Harvest Books) (Harcourt)
Paris France (Liveright)
Picasso (Beacon Press)
Tender Buttons (Haskell House Pubs.)
Three Lives (Vintage)
What Are Masterpieces (Pitman)
The World is Round (Camelot Books) (Avon)

For Further Reading

The following books deal either directly with Gertrude Stein and her writings or with the period in which she lived.

Bridgman, Richard. *Gertrude Stein in Pieces.* New York: Oxford University Press, 1971.

Brinnin, John Malcolm. *The Third Rose: Gertrude Stein and Her World.* Boston: Little, Brown, 1959.

Flanner, Janet. *Paris Was Yesterday.* New York: The Viking Press, 1972.

Four Americans in Paris. New York: The Museum of Modern Art, 1971.

Fuller, Edmund, ed. *Journey into the Self: Being the Letters, Papers and Journals of Leo Stein.* New York: Crown Publishers, 1950.

Gallup, Donald, ed. *The Flowers of Friendship: Letters to Gertrude Stein.* New York: Alfred A. Knopf, 1953.

Haas, Robert B., ed. *A Primer for the Gradual Understanding of Gertrude Stein.* Los Angeles: Black Sparrow, 1972.

Hemingway, Ernest. *A Moveable Feast.* New York: Charles Scribner's Sons, 1964.

Housman, John. *Run-Through.* New York: Simon and Schuster, 1972.

Rogers, W. G. *When This You See Remember Me.* New York: Rinehart & Co., 1948.

Sprigge, Elizabeth. *Gertrude Stein: Her Life and Her Work.* New York: Harper & Brothers, 1957.

Sutherland, Donald. *Gertrude Stein: A Biography of Her Work.* New Haven: Yale University Press, 1951.

Thomson, Virgil. *Virgil Thomson.* New York: Alfred A. Knopf, 1966.

Toklas, Alice B. *What is Remembered.* New York: Holt, Rinehart & Winston, Inc., 1963.

Wilson, Edmund. *Axel's Castle.* New York: Charles Scribner's Sons, 1931.

Photocredits

The author wishes to acknowledge for use of photographs:

The Bettmann Archive, Inc: 30, 108, 114
Brown Brothers: 14, 85, 90
Estate of Carl Van Vechten: 67, 124, 131
Pictorial Parade: frontispiece, 83, 92
Yale University, The Beinecke Rare Book and Manuscript Library,
Collection of American Literature: 5, 10, 19, 24, 32, 34, 37, 39, 44,
64, 65, 76, 94 (photograph by Man Ray), 95, 96 (photograph by Man
Ray), 118, 126, 127, 133, 134, 139

Index

ABOUT THE AUTHOR

HOWARD GREENFELD was born and raised in New York City. He attended the University of Chicago, New York University, and Columbia University, from which he received his M.A. In addition to publishing a great many books under his own Orion Press imprint, he is the author of *Picasso, Marc Chagall,* and *The Impressionist Revolution.* Mr. Greenfeld now edits a list under his own name for J. Philip O'Hara and divides his time between New York City, Paris, and Italy.